Common Core
Standards Practice
Workbook

Grade 2

Teacher Guide

Glenview, Illinois • Boston, Massachusetts
Chandler, Arizona • Upper Saddle River, New Jersey

ALWAYS LEARNING

PEARSON

Grade 2 Contents

 **Standards Practice**

 **Assessment**

 **Teacher Support**

About this Guide

Pearson is pleased to offer this **Common Core Standards Practice** Teacher's Guide, a companion to the **Common Core Standards Practice Workbook.** It includes these pages:

- **Common Core Standards Practice pages.** Two pages of practice exercises for each Common Core State Standard. Students will find different kinds of exercises that are similar to the items expected to be on the Next Generation Assessment that students will be taking starting in 2014–2015.

- **Practice for the Common Core Assessment.** Each Practice Assessment consists of one (1) Practice End-of-Year Assessment and two (2) Performance Tasks. One Practice Assessment is found in the Student Workbook, while the second is a "secure" test found only in this Teacher's Guide. The two Practice End-of-Year Assessments are mirror assessments.

  The Practice End-of-Year assessment was built to align to the content emphases of both PARCC and SBAC. That means that 70% of the items assess major content emphases. In addition, many of the items are similar to the innovative items that are expected to be on the upcoming Next Generation Assessments. Students will encounter multiple-response selected-response items; simulated technology-enabled items that ask students to sort answer options into appropriate categories or to construct responses on grids, graphs, and number lines; constructed response items that ask them to explain their reasoning or justify their thinking; and extended constructed response items that include multi-part questions with multi-step solutions. The Performance Tasks present students with problem situations in real-world context and ask students to make use of their developing proficiency with the Standards for Mathematical Practice and their firmer understanding of Math Content to find solutions.

- Answers to all of the student pages as 4-ups.

- **Correlation Chart for the Practice EOY Assessment.** The chart indicates for each item the Content Standard assessed and lessons in *enVisionMATH™ Common Core* and sessions in *Investigations in Number, Data, and Space® for the Common Core* where students can go for more practice of the standard assessed.

- **Scoring Rubrics for the four (4) Performance Tasks.** In addition to recommendations for scoring, these pages list both the Standards for Mathematical Practice and Mathematical Content that the task assesses.

Common Core Standards Practice and Assessments

Name _____

Common Core Standards Practice

2.OA.1 Use addition and subtraction within 100 to solve one- and two-step word problems involving situations of adding to, taking from, putting together, taking apart, and comparing, with unknowns in all positions, e.g., by using drawings and equations with a symbol for the unknown number to represent the problem.

I. Samantha has 6 toy cars.
Roger has 10 toy cars.
How many do they have in all?

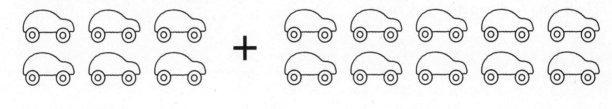

_____

....

2. Tim has 29 stickers.
Maya has 14 fewer stickers than Tim.
Draw a model to match the story problem.

How many stickers does Maya have?

_____

3. Emma has 53 marbles.
She gets some marbles from Fred.
Then she gives 10 marbles to Tessie.
She now has 58 marbles.
How many marbles does she get from Fred?

Write a number sentence to solve.
Use ? for the unknown.

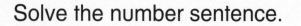

Solve the number sentence.

_____

4. Allison buys 25 roses and some tulips.
She loses 4 flowers on her way home.
At home, she counts 30 flowers.
How many tulips did she buy?

Draw a model to match the story problem.

Solve the number sentence.

_____

Name _____

Common Core Standards Practice

2.OA.2 Fluently add and subtract within 20 using mental strategies. By end of Grade 2, know from memory all sums of two one-digit numbers.

Solve.

1. 7 + 12 = ☐

　Ⓐ 20

　Ⓑ 19

　Ⓒ 12

　Ⓓ 15

2. 8 + 9 = ☐

　Ⓐ 20

　Ⓑ 19

　Ⓒ 17

　Ⓓ 15

3. 13 − 7 = ☐

_____

4. 13 + 6 = ☐

_____

5. 14 − 6 = ☐

_____

6. 19 − 5 = ☐

_____

7. $18 - 9 =$ ☐

(A) 7

(B) 8

(C) 9

(D) 10

8. $12 - 9 =$ ☐

(A) 3

(B) 4

(C) 5

(D) 6

9. $15 - 6 =$ ☐

_____

10. $4 + 16 =$ ☐

_____

11. $5 + 12 =$ ☐

_____

12. $13 + 7 =$ ☐

_____

CC 4

Name _____

Common Core Standards Practice

2.OA.3 Determine whether a group of objects (up to 20) has an odd or even number of members, e.g., by pairing objects or counting them by 2s; write an equation to express an even number as a sum of two equal addends.

1. Which shows an odd number of strawberries?

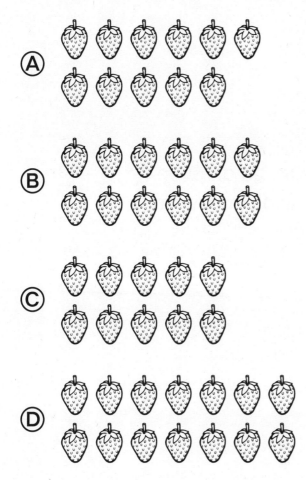

---

2. Tom has 14 marbles.

Kara has 15 marbles.

Who has an even number of marbles?

_____

Explain how you know with words or a model.

3. Which equation shows 12 as the sum of two even numbers?

Ⓐ $2 \times 6 = 12$

Ⓑ $8 + 8 = 12$

Ⓒ $5 + 7 = 12$

Ⓓ $6 + 6 = 12$

4. Leo adds 4 and 4. Will the sum be an even number or an odd number? Explain how you know using words or a model.

Name _____

Common Core Standards Practice

2.OA.4 Use addition to find the total number of objects arranged in rectangular arrays with up to 5 rows and up to 5 columns; write an equation to express the total as a sum of equal addends.

1. Look at the apples.

Write an equation to show the number of apples.

_____ + _____ + _____ = _____

2. Look at the pears.

Write an equation to show the number of pears.

_____ + _____ + _____ + _____ = _____

3.

Write an equation to show the number of mugs.

____ ◯ ____ ◯ ____

4.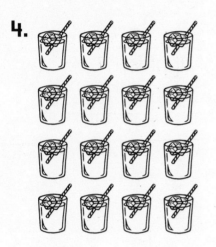

Write an equation to show the number of glasses.

____ ◯ ____ ◯ ____ ◯ ____ ◯ ____

5.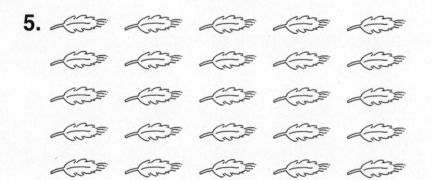

Write an equation to show the number of feathers.

____ ◯ ____ ◯ ____ ◯ ____ ◯ ____ ◯ ____

Name _____

Common Core Standards Practice

2.NBT.1 Understand that the three digits of a three-digit number represent amounts of hundreds, tens, and ones; e.g., 706 equals 7 hundreds, 0 tens, and 6 ones. Understand the following as special cases: **a.** 100 can be thought of as a bundle of ten tens — called a "hundred." **b.** The numbers 100, 200, 300, 400, 500, 600, 700, 800, 900 refer to one, two, three, four, five, six, seven, eight, or nine hundreds (and 0 tens and 0 ones).

1. What is the value of the digit 3 in the number 392?

- Ⓐ 3
- Ⓑ 30
- Ⓒ 300
- Ⓓ 390

2. What is the value of the digit 7 in the number 117?

- Ⓐ 1
- Ⓑ 7
- Ⓒ 70
- Ⓓ 700

3. Complete the number sentence:

124 = _____ + 20 + 4

4. How many hundreds are there in 864? Explain how you know.

5. How many tens are in 182?

Ⓐ 8

Ⓑ 10

Ⓒ 80

Ⓓ 800

6. What is the value of the digit 6 in the number 604?

Ⓐ 6

Ⓑ 60

Ⓒ 600

Ⓓ 660

7. Complete the number sentence.

242 = 200 + _____ + 2

8. Look at the number 123.

a. What is the value of each digit in the number?

b. Write the number as a sum of the numbers in its three place values.

Name _____

Common Core Standards Practice

2.NBT.2 Count within 1000; skip-count by 5s, 10s, and 100s.

1. Count by 10s. Which number comes next?

60, 70, 80, 90, _____

Ⓐ 99

Ⓑ 100

Ⓒ 900

Ⓓ 990

2. Count by 100s. Which number comes next?

400, 500, 600, 700, _____

Ⓐ 100

Ⓑ 800

Ⓒ 900

Ⓓ 999

3. Count by 5s. What number comes next?

80, 85, 90, 95, _____

4. Count by 100s. What number comes next?

200, 300, 400, 500, _____

5. Fill in the missing numbers.

880, 890, _____, 910, _____

6. Fill in the missing numbers.

450, _____, 650, 750, _____

7. What number comes next?

345, 350, 355, 360, _____

8. Jeremy skips-counts by 100 to 1000.
Which number does he NOT say?

Ⓐ 300

Ⓑ 700

Ⓒ 910

Ⓓ 1000

CC 12

Name _____

Common Core Standards Practice

2.NBT.3 Read and write numbers to 1000 using base-ten numerals, number names, and expanded form.

1. Which number is two hundred eighty-nine?

(A) 892

(B) 298

(C) 289

(D) 829

2. Which number is one hundred sixty-four?

(A) 146

(B) 614

(C) 164

(D) 416

Match the numerals with the names. Not all of the numbers have matches.

3. Two hundred fifty   202

4. Seven hundred sixteen   932

5. Nine hundred thirty-two   329

6. Two hundred two   760

7. Seven hundred sixty   525

8. Five hundred twenty-five   225

                                                        716

9. Which equals 516?

    Ⓐ 51 + 6

    Ⓑ 500 + 10 + 6

    Ⓒ 500 + 16 + 6

    Ⓓ 5 + 16

10. Which equals 228?

    Ⓐ 22 + 8

    Ⓑ 2 + 28

    Ⓒ 200 + 82

    Ⓓ 200 + 20 + 8

Complete each equation by writing the number in expanded form.

11. 347 = _____ + 40 + 7

12. 166 = _____ + _____ + _____

13. 801 = _____ + _____ + _____

14. 450 = _____ + _____ + _____

15. 279 = _____ + _____ + _____

16. 912 = _____ + _____ + _____

Common Core Standards Practice

2.NBT.4 Compare two three-digit numbers based on meanings of the hundreds, tens, and ones digits, using >, =, and < symbols to record the results of comparisons.

1. Which symbol goes in the circle to make the inequality true?

131 ◯ 129

(A) >

(B) =

(C) <

(D) +

2. Which symbol goes in the circle to make the inequality true?

448 ◯ 484

(A) >

(B) =

(C) <

(D) ×

Complete each inequality. Tell with words or a model how you know which number is greater.

3. 356 ◯ 401

4. 512 ◯ 509

CC 15

5. Which statement compares 923 and 899?

Ⓐ 923 > 899

Ⓑ 923 < 899

Ⓒ 923 = 899

Ⓓ 923 + 899

6. Which statement compares 167 and 170?

Ⓐ 170 > 167

Ⓑ 170 < 167

Ⓒ 170 = 167

Ⓓ 170 × 167

Complete each inequality. Tell with words or a model how you know which number is less.

7. 772 ◯ 687

8. 513 ◯ 531

Name _____

Common Core Standards Practice

2.NBT.5 Fluently add and subtract within 100 using strategies based on place value, properties of operations, and/or the relationship between addition and subtraction.

Solve.

1. 16
    + 33

2. 89
    − 63

3. 32
    − 13

4. 46
    + 38

5. 48
    + 43

6. 56
    − 47

CC 17

7. 82 − 28 = ☐

8. 73 + 18 = ☐

9. 28 + 74 = ☐

10. 41 − 36 = ☐

11. 96 − 44 = ☐

12. 67 + 76 = ☐

Name _____

Common Core Standards Practice

2.NBT.6 Add up to four two-digit numbers using strategies based on place value and properties of operations.

1. Dana has 12 apples.
She also has 14 mangoes and 16 oranges.
How many pieces of fruit does she have in all?

Ⓐ 25   Ⓑ 30   Ⓒ 42   Ⓓ 50

2. Aisha will find the sum of these numbers.

$20 + 22 + 10 + 14 =$ ☐

Which two numbers would you add first?
Tell why.

What is the sum?

_____

3. Paul finds the sum of these numbers.

$30 + 21 + 11 =$ ☐

He adds $30 + 20 + 10$, then adds 2. Is his sum
correct? Tell how you know.

4. Monica collects stickers.
She has 30 cat stickers, 30 butterfly stickers,
and 12 flower stickers.
How many stickers does she have in all?

Ⓐ 60

Ⓑ 75

Ⓒ 80

Ⓓ 72

5. Tell how you can find the sum of these
numbers. You can use words or models.

$$15 + 18 + 20 + 25 = \boxed{}$$

What is the sum?

_____

6. Find the sum:

$$23 + 18 + 17 = \boxed{}$$

_____

Name _____

Common Core Standards Practice

2.NBT.7 Add and subtract within 1000, using concrete models or drawings and strategies based on place value, properties of operations, and/or the relationship between addition and subtraction; relate the strategy to a written method. Understand that in adding or subtracting three digit numbers, one adds or subtracts hundreds and hundreds, tens and tens, ones and ones; and sometimes it is necessary to compose or decompose tens or hundreds.

I. Elise has 721 gold coins and 236 silver coins.
How many coins does she have in all?

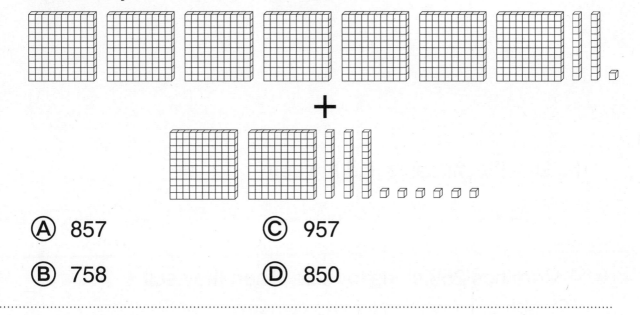

   Ⓐ 857   Ⓒ 957

   Ⓑ 758   Ⓓ 850

- -

2. There are 356 people at a show. Then 171
people leave. How many people are left?
You can use the model to find the difference.

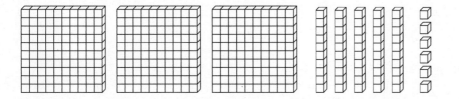

_____

3. Jason's father builds a wall with 542 bricks.
Jason adds 289 bricks.
How many bricks do they use in all?

   a. Draw a model to show the sum.

   b. Use the model to find the sum.

   _____

4. A store has 253 shirts for sale. Then they sell
190 shirts. How many shirts remain?

   a. Draw a model to show the difference.

   b. Use the model to find the difference.

   _____

Name _____

Common Core Standards Practice

2.NBT.8 Mentally add 10 or 100 to a given number 100–900, and mentally subtract 10 or 100 from a given number 100–900.

Find these sums or differences.

1. 290 − 10 = ☐

    Ⓐ 300

    Ⓑ 250

    Ⓒ 280

    Ⓓ 260

2. 390 + 10 = ☐

    Ⓐ 300

    Ⓑ 400

    Ⓒ 380

    Ⓓ 410

3.

470 + 10 = ☐ _____

4.

970 − 10 = ☐ _____

5.

800 − 10 = ☐ _____

CC 23

Find these sums or differences.

6. 690 − 100 = ☐

   Ⓐ 590

   Ⓑ 680

   Ⓒ 700

   Ⓓ 600

7. 430 + 100 = ☐

   Ⓐ 330

   Ⓑ 440

   Ⓒ 530

   Ⓓ 500

8.
470 + 100 = ☐ _____

9.
770 − 100 = ☐ _____

10.
180 − 100 = ☐ _____

Name _____

Common Core Standards Practice

2.NBT.9 Explain why addition and subtraction strategies work, using place value and the properties of operations.

1. Jeff adds these two numbers.

$$349$$
$$+\ \ 22$$

a. Can he add 3 and 2? Tell why.

b. What is the sum? _____

2. Tell two different ways to find the sum.
You can use words or models.

$$253$$
$$+\,706$$

One way:

Another way:

3. Juan subtracts these two numbers.

357
− 194

a. What must he do to subtract the numbers in the tens place?

_____

_____

b. What is the difference? _____

4. Tell two different ways to find the difference.

414
− 178

One way:

_____

_____

Another way:

_____

_____

c. What is the difference? _____

Name _____

Common Core Standards Practice

2.MD.1. Measure the length of an object by selecting and using appropriate tools such as rulers, yardsticks, meter sticks, and measuring tapes.

1. Ahmed will measure the length of his book in inches. Which tool should he use? Tell why he should use that tool.

....

2. How long in inches is this crayon? Use an inch ruler to measure the length.

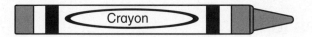

The crayon is _____ long.

....

3. Roger's father will measure the length of the family car. What tool should he use? Tell why.

4. How long is the rope? Use an inch ruler to measure its length.

The rope is _____ inches long.

....

5. Jeannie's mother needs to measure the width of the windows in the living room. What tool should she use to measure the width? Tell why.

....

6. How long is this figure?
Measure the figure in inches.

The figure is _____ inches long.

Name _____

Common Core Standards Practice

2.MD.2 Measure the length of an object twice, using length units of different lengths for the two measurements; describe how the two measurements relate to the size of the unit chosen.

1. Use a centimeter straight edge or meter stick to make these measurements.

   a. How wide is one window in the classroom? Measure in centimeters. Then measure in meters.

      The window is _____ centimeters wide.

      The window is _____ meters wide.

   b. Which measurement is greater?

   c. Which unit is larger?

....

2. Use an inch ruler or a yardstick to make these measurements.

   a. How wide is the classroom door? Measure in inches. Then measure in feet.

      The door is _____ inches wide.

      The door is _____ feet wide.

   b. Which measurement is greater?

   c. Which unit is larger?

CC 29

The children in Mrs. Peters' class made measurements in their classroom. Circle the most likely unit for each measurement.

3. the width of the chalkboard

2 (centimeters, meters)

4. the length of a crayon

10 (centimeters, meters)

5. the height of the room

220 (centimeters, meters)

6. the length of a pencil

5 (inches, feet)

7. the height of a child

3 (inches, feet)

8. the width of a computer screen

15 (inches, feet)

Name _____

Common Core Standards Practice

2.MD.3 Estimate lengths using units of inches, feet, centimeters, and meters.

Circle the best estimate for these lengths.

1. the height of a chair

    3 inches   10 inches   25 inches

....

2. the length of a crayon

    4 inches   12 inches   32 inches

....

3. the width of a child's desk

    2 inches   20 inches   200 inches

....

4. the length of a school bus

    2 feet   38 feet   380 feet

....

5. the height of a house with 2 floors

    3 feet   10 feet   30 feet

CC 31

Circle the best estimate for these lengths.

6. the width of a chair

4 centimeters   40 centimeters   400 centimeters

7. the width of a bracelet

1 centimeter   7 centimeters   30 centimeters

8. the height of a bottle of juice

14 centimeters   60 centimeters   100 centimeters

9. the height of an adult

2 meters   10 meters   20 meters

10. the length of a driveway to a house

2 meters   15 meters   600 meters

Name _____

Common Core Standards Practice

2.MD.4 Measure to determine how much longer one object is than another, expressing the length difference in terms of a standard length unit.

1. Use a centimeter ruler to measure these two pencils.

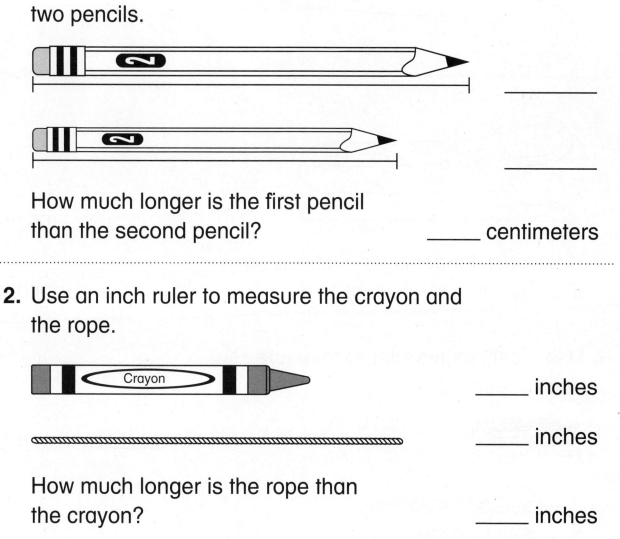

_____

_____

How much longer is the first pencil than the second pencil?

_____ centimeters

2. Use an inch ruler to measure the crayon and the rope.

_____ inches

_____ inches

How much longer is the rope than the crayon?

_____ inches

3. Use an inch ruler to measure each scissors.

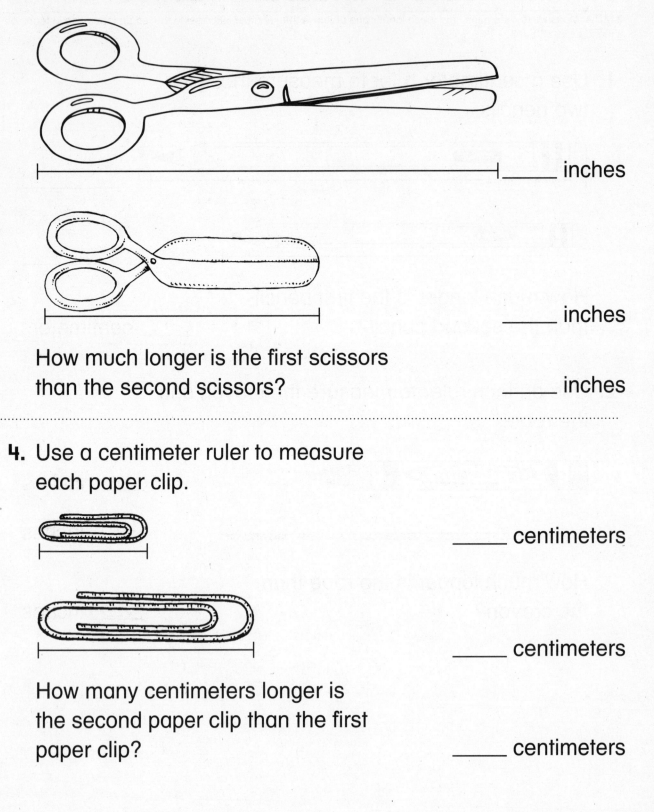

_____ inches

_____ inches

How much longer is the first scissors
than the second scissors?

_____ inches

4. Use a centimeter ruler to measure
each paper clip.

_____ centimeters

_____ centimeters

How many centimeters longer is
the second paper clip than the first
paper clip?

_____ centimeters

Name _____

Common Core Standards Practice

2.MD.5 Use addition and subtraction within 100 to solve word problems involving lengths that are given in the same units, e.g., by using drawings (such as drawings of rulers) and equations with a symbol for the unknown number to represent the problem.

1. Monica's table is 41 centimeters long.
Rebecca's table is 12 centimeters shorter
than Monica's.
How long is Rebecca's table?

Ⓐ 27 centimeters

Ⓑ 29 centimeters

Ⓒ 36 centimeters

Ⓓ 39 centimeters

2. Ellie has two pieces of ribbon. One piece is
27 inches. The other piece is 15 inches.

a. Draw a model to match the problem.

b. How many inches of ribbon does Ellie have?

_____

3. Jacob walks 65 meters from his classroom to the library. Then he walks 25 meters to the gym. How far does he walk?

Use the number line to show how far Jacobs walks.

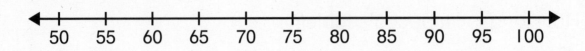

Write an equation to match the problem.

How far does Jacob walk?

_____

4. A hot air balloon is 93 feet above the ground. Then it drops 75 feet. How far above the ground is it now?

Write an equation to match the problem.

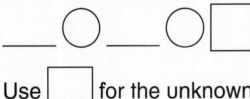

Use ☐ for the unknown.

How high above the ground is the balloon?

_____

Name _____

Common Core Standards Practice

2.MD.6 Represent whole numbers as lengths from 0 on a number line diagram with equally spaced points corresponding to the numbers 0, 1, 2, ..., and represent whole-number sums and differences within 100 on a number line diagram.

1. Pencil A is 3 inches long.
   Pencil B is 5 inches long.
   Pencil C is 8 inches long.
   Write A, B, and C on the number line to show each length.

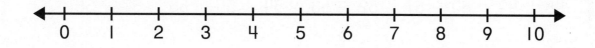

2. Use the number line below to represent this addition number sentence.

$$45 + 6 = \boxed{}$$

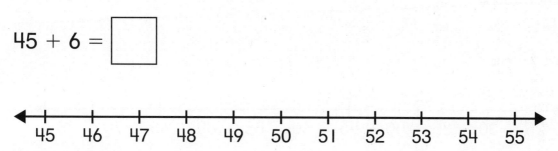

Use the number line to represent these number sentences.

3. 42 − 6

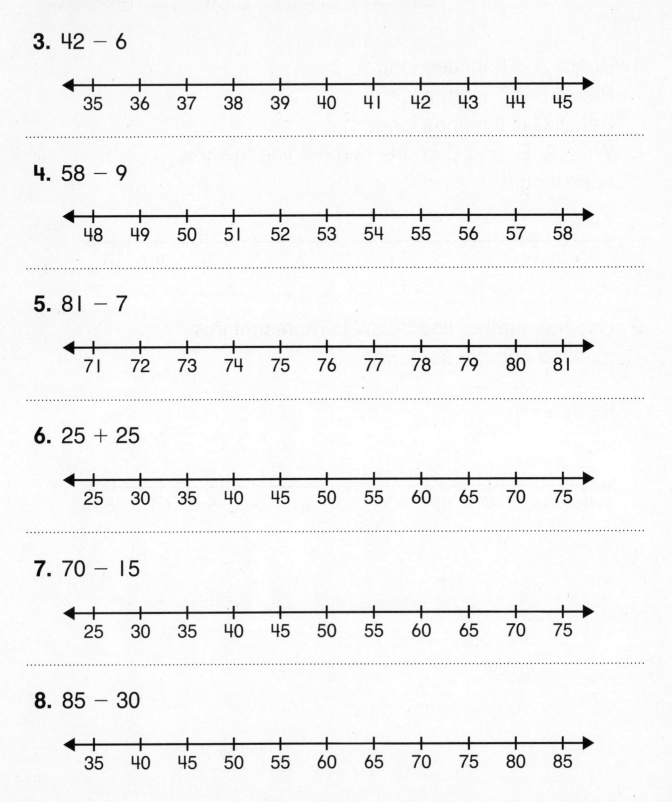

4. 58 − 9

5. 81 − 7

6. 25 + 25

7. 70 − 15

8. 85 − 30

Name _____

Common Core Standards Practice

2.MD.7 Tell and write time from analog and digital clocks to the nearest five minutes, using a.m. and p.m.

1. The clock shows the time that Joel's father
wakes up every morning.

What time does Joel's father wake up?
Use A.M. or P.M.

_____ : _____

....

2. Sadie gets home from school every afternoon
at the time shown on the clock below.

What time does Sadie get home from school?
Use A.M. or P.M.

_____ : _____

3. Math class begins after lunch.
The clock shows the time.

What time does math class begin?
Use A.M. or P.M.

_____ : _____

....

4. Mr. Jenkins comes home late one evening.
The clock shows the time.

What time does Mr. Jenkins come home?
Use A.M. or P.M.

_____ : _____

Name _____

Common Core Standards Practice

2.MD.8 Solve word problems involving dollar bills, quarters, dimes, nickels, and pennies, using $ and ¢ symbols appropriately. Example: If you have 2 dimes and 3 pennies, how many cents do you have?

1. Becky has the coins shown.
How much money does she have?

_____ ¢

. . . .

2. Rosaline has three $1 bills, 1 quarter,
and 3 dimes.
How much money does she have?

_____

3. Jill has 87 ¢. Which set of coins could
she have?

Ⓐ

Ⓑ

Ⓒ

Ⓓ

....

4. Abe has two $1 bills, 3 quarters, and 1 nickel.
How much money does Abe have in all?

_____

2

Common Core Standards Practice

2.MD.9 Generate measurement data by measuring lengths of several objects to the nearest whole unit, or by making repeated measurements of the same object. Show the measurements by making a line plot, where the horizontal scale is marked off in whole-number units.

1. Measure with an inch ruler 5 pencils.
Write the length of each pencil in the table.

Pencil	Length (inches)
1	
2	
3	
4	
5	

2. Put each measurement on the line plot.

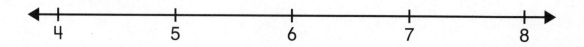

4   5   6   7   8

3. Measure with a centimeter ruler 5 books.
   Write the length of each book in the table.

Book	Length (centimeters)
1	
2	
3	
4	
5	

4. Put each measurement on the line plot.

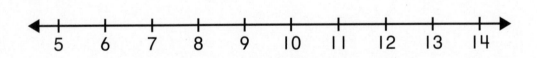

Name _____

Common Core Standards Practice

2.MD.10 Draw a picture graph and a bar graph (with single-unit scale) to represent a data set with up to four categories. Solve simple put-together, take-apart, and compare problems using information presented in a bar graph.

The table shows the number of books four students read this week.

Club Member	Number of Books
Judy	5
Eric	3
LaToya	2
Juan	4

1. Make a picture graph to show the data in the table.

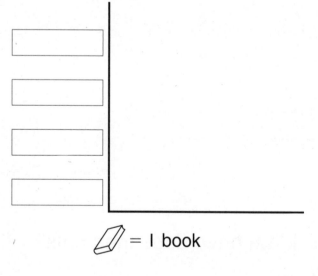

= 1 book

....

2. How many books did the four students read this week?

_____

The table shows the pets that the children in one class have.

Pet	Number of children
Bird	5
Cat	7
Dog	12
Hamster	3

3. Fill in the bar graph to match the data in the table.

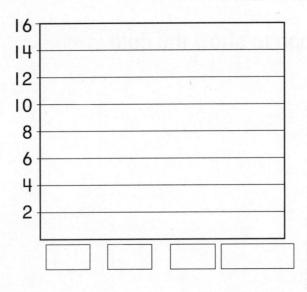

4. How many more children have dogs than cats? Tell how you know.

_____

Name _____

Common Core Standards Practice

2.G.1 Recognize and draw shapes having specified attributes, such as a given number of angles or a given number of equal faces. Identify triangles, quadrilaterals, pentagons, hexagons, and cubes.

I. Write the letter *Q* inside each shape that is a quadrilateral.

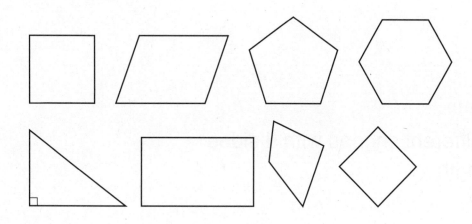

....

2. Name these shapes.

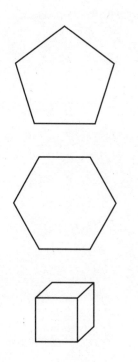

_____

_____

_____

3. Draw a shape with 3 sides of equal length.

- -

4. Draw two different shapes with 4 sides of equal length.

- -

5. Draw a shape with 5 angles.

Name _____

Common Core Standards Practice

2.G.2 Partition a rectangle into rows and columns of same-size squares and count to find the total number of them.

I.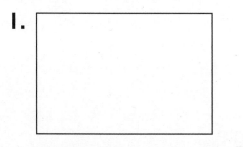

   a. Draw a line across the rectangle to make two smaller rectangles, each of the same size.

   b. Draw two lines to divide the rectangles into equal-sized squares.

   c. How many squares did you make? _____

----

2. Divide the rectangle into 8 squares.

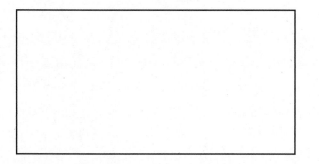

3.

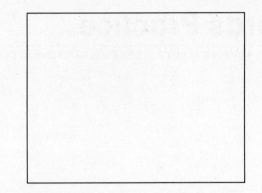

   a. Draw two lines across the rectangle to make three smaller rectangles, each of the same size.

   b. Draw three lines to divide the rectangles into squares.

   c. How many squares did you make? _____

---

4. Divide the rectangle into 15 squares.

Name _____

Common Core Standards Practice

2.G.3 Partition circles and rectangles into two, three, or four equal shares, describe the shares using the words halves, thirds, half of, a third of, etc., and describe the whole as two halves, three thirds, four fourths. Recognize that equal shares of identical wholes need not have the same shape.

1.

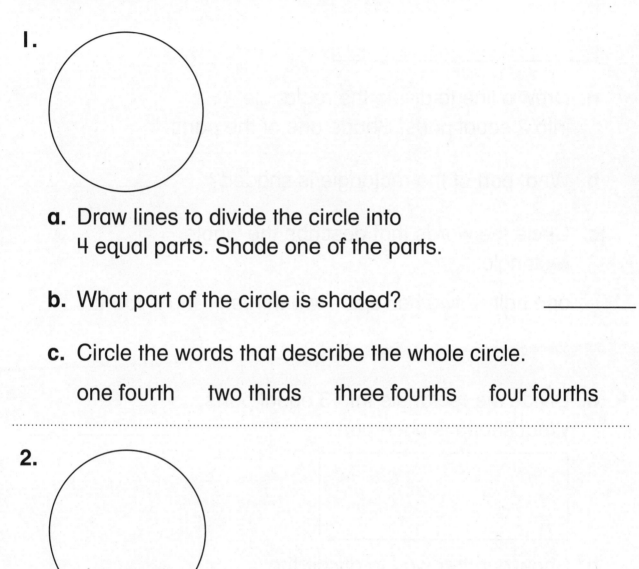

a. Draw lines to divide the circle into 4 equal parts. Shade one of the parts.

b. What part of the circle is shaded? _____

c. Circle the words that describe the whole circle.

   one fourth   two thirds   three fourths   four fourths

2.

a. Draw lines to divide the circle into 3 equal parts. Shade one of the parts.

b. What part of the circle is shaded? _____

c. Circle the words that describe the whole circle.

   one third   one half   two thirds   three thirds

3.

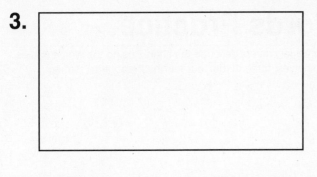

a. Draw a line to divide the rectangle into 2 equal parts. Shade one of the parts.

b. What part of the rectangle is shaded? _____

c. Circle the words that describe the whole rectangle.

one half   two halves   two thirds   three fourths

---

4. a. Divide the rectangle into 3 equal parts. What shape is each part? _____

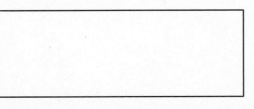

b. Show another way to divide the rectangle into 3 equal parts. What shape is each part? _____

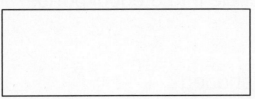

Name _____

Practice End-of-Year Assessment

I. Henry has two pieces of cloth. One piece is 12 inches long. The other is 25 inches long. How many inches of cloth does Henry have if he puts the two pieces together?

....

2. About how wide is the board in your classroom?

....

3. What is the value of the digit 2 in the number 324?

4. Find the sum of these numbers.

$$12 + 20 + 14 + 16 = \boxed{}$$

---

5. How many hundreds are in 724?

(A) 2

(B) 4

(C) 7

(D) 24

---

6. Jacob wants to measure the length
of his shoe.
What tool can he use?

7. Emily has 85 sheets of construction paper. She uses 34 sheets for a project. How many sheets of paper does Emily have left?

8. Draw a model to show 456 minus 173. Then find the difference.

_____

9. Andrew has a piece of string that is 82 inches long. Then he cuts 15 inches off the end of the string. How long is Andrew's string now?

10. Morrie measures the stem of a flower. It is 12 inches long. Aisha also measures the stem of the same flower. She finds it is 1 foot long.

a. Why do Morrie and Aisha have different heights for the same stem?

b. In a measurement of height, is the number of inches less than, equal to, or greater than the number of feet? How do you know?

11. Solve.

$$
\begin{array}{r}
34 \\
-19 \\
\hline
\end{array}
$$

12. Andrew has the coins shown below.

How much money, in cents, does he have in all?

. . . .

13. Julia read 510 pages. Jack read 479 pages.

Who read more pages? Tell how you know. Use a model or a number sentence to show.

14. A teacher arranges desks into 4 rows of 3.

Draw a model to match the desks.

How many desks are there?

15. Find the sum.

$$32 + 47 + 54 = \boxed{}$$

16. Mark has 42 marbles in one pile. He has 16 marbles in another pile. Draw a model to show the total number of marbles, and find the total.

17. Lucy's ribbon is 24 centimeters long.
Sarah's ribbon is 18 centimeters long.
How much longer is Lucy's ribbon?

18. Write the number 751 in expanded form.

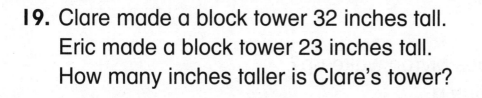

19. Clare made a block tower 32 inches tall.
Eric made a block tower 23 inches tall.
How many inches taller is Clare's tower?

20. Use the number line to show 23 − 6.

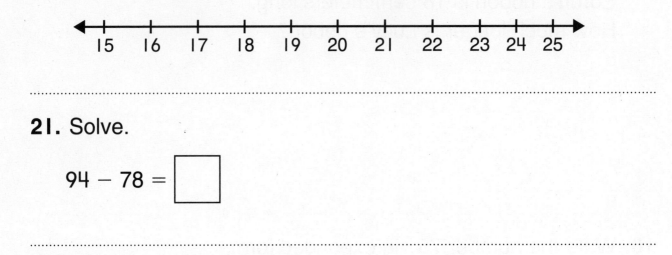

$$15 \quad 16 \quad 17 \quad 18 \quad 19 \quad 20 \quad 21 \quad 22 \quad 23 \quad 24 \quad 25$$

21. Solve.

$$94 - 78 = \boxed{}$$

22. Myron wakes up in the morning at the time shown on the clock.

What time does Myron wake up?
Include A.M. or P.M.

23. Divide the circle into 3 equal parts.

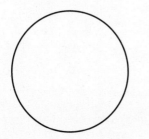

24. Use the number line to show the sum of 43 and 8.

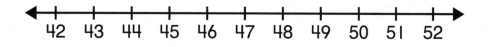

25. In a computer game, James scores
825 points. Erin scores 100 points more
than James. What is Erin's score?

26. Write the letter "P" inside the pentagon.

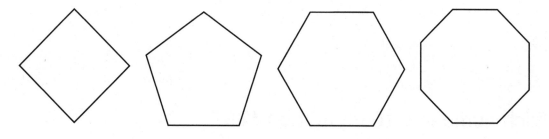

27.

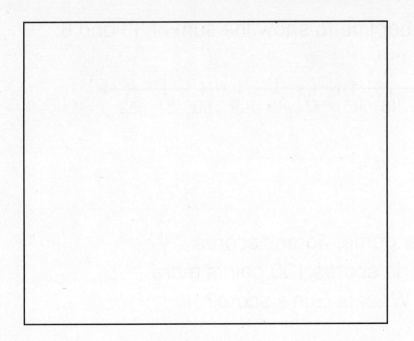

   a. Draw three lines across the rectangle to make four smaller rectangles, each the same size.

   b. Draw four lines to divide the rectangles into squares.

   c. How many squares did you make?

---

28. Which number is 10 more than 678?

   Ⓐ   688

   Ⓑ   668

   Ⓒ   778

   Ⓓ   578

29. Joy has 46 cents in her pocket.
She has 25 cents in her hand.
How many cents does Joy have in all?

· ·

30. Adam arranges oranges in the arrangement
shown below.

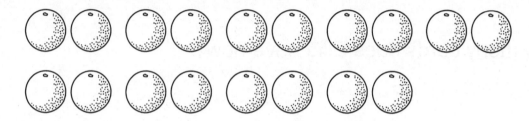

Does he have an even or odd number
of oranges? Tell how you know.

· ·

31. Find the next number in this sequence.
740, 750, 760, 770, _____

32. Ellie has 342 cards.
Sandra gives her 175 cards.

Draw a model to match the story problem.

How many cards does Ellie have now?

....

33. Draw a model to show this subtraction problem:

63 − 35

34. Which group does each figure belong? Write the letter of the figure in the correct box.

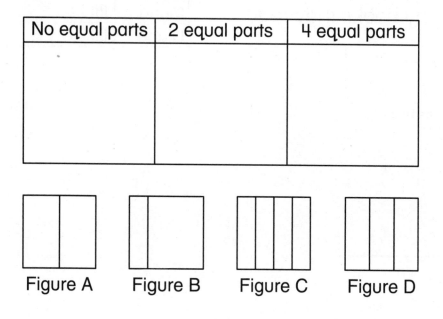

No equal parts	2 equal parts	4 equal parts

Figure A   Figure B   Figure C   Figure D

. . . .

35. Emma divides the rectangle into 3 equal rows and 4 equal columns. How many squares are in the rectangle?

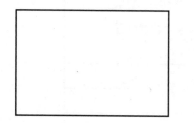

36. Pamela and her friends count the books that they read. The tally chart shows how many books they read.

Number of Books

Pamela	IIII I
Maria	IIII I
Diane	IIII

Complete the pictograph to match the tally chart.

Books Read

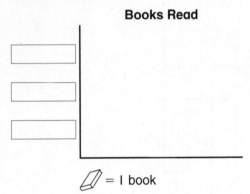

▱ = 1 book

---

37. Mia rolled a number cube 10 times. The table shows the results.

Number on cube	Number of times the number was rolled
1	1
2	2
3	2
4	0
5	3
6	2

Draw Xs to show Mia's results on a line plot.

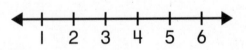

38. Find the sum.

$12 + 85 = \boxed{}$

---

39. Complete each inequality. Tell with words or a model how you know which number is less.

349 _____ 352

531 _____ 513

---

40. Which of these is equal to 16? Circle Yes or No

9 + 7   Yes   No

6 + 12   Yes   No

11 + 4   Yes   No

8 + 8   Yes   No

Name _____

Performance Task 1

Part A

Claire and her classmates are selling boxes of oranges. The table shows how many boxes of oranges they were sold in Weeks 1 and 2.

Boxes of Oranges Sold	
Week 1	27
Week 2	43

Claire wants to know how many boxes of oranges they sold in all.

1. How Claire can find the number of boxes of oranges they sold in week 1 and week 2. Show two ways to find the answer. Use pictures, numbers, or words.

Part B

One customer asks Claire how many oranges are in one box. Claire opens a box and this is what she sees.

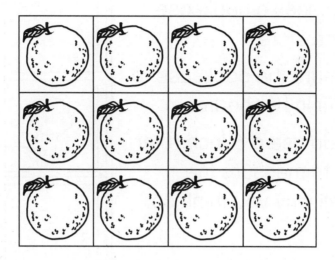

2. How can Claire find the number of oranges in a box?

3. How many oranges are in a box?

4. Is the number of oranges in a box an even or odd number? Tell how you know.

Name _____

Performance Task 2

Part A

Amanda will get a new bookcase for her bedroom. She sees a bookcase that she likes at the store.

Amanda will measure the bookcase to make sure it can fit in her bedroom.

1. Should Amanda use a 6-inch ruler or a yardstick to measure the bookcase? Tell why you think so.

Part B

The shelves in the bookcase are 16 inches high. Amanda wants to make sure her books will fit in the bookcase.

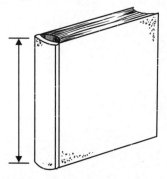

2. Find three different books in your classroom and measure their height.

   Book 1: _____ Book 2: _____ Book 3: _____

3. Which books that you measured will fit in Amanda's bookcase?

   Explain how you know which books will fit.

Name _____

Practice End-of-Year Assessment
Test 2

1. Eli is 39 inches tall. His brother Jack is
  11 inches taller than Eli. How tall is Jack?

....

2. About how long is your pen or pencil.
  Use units of centimeters.

....

3. What is the value of the digit 3 in the
  number 394?

4. Find the sum of these numbers.

$$18 + 17 + 12 + 10 = \underline{\hspace{2cm}}$$

....

5. How many tens are in 914?

Ⓐ 1

Ⓑ 4

Ⓒ 9

Ⓓ 14

....

6. Jane wants to measure the width of her book.

What tool can she use?

7. There are 64 fish in a large tank. The owner moves 18 of the fish into a smaller tank. How many fish are left in the large tank?

8. Draw a model to show 436 minus 165. Then find the difference.

9. Molly has a length of string 47 centimeters long. Then she cuts 19 centimeters off the end of the string. How long is Molly's string now?

10. Maria measures the length of a hallway. It is 9 feet long. Franks also measures the length of the hallway. He finds it is 3 yards long.

    a. Why do Maria and Frank have different lengths for the same hallway?

    b. In a measurement of length, is the number of feet less than, equal to, or greater than the number of yards? How do you know?

- -

11. Solve.

$$\begin{array}{r} 56 \\ -17 \\ \hline \end{array}$$

12. Stella has the coins shown below.

How much money, in cents, does she have in all?

---

13. Anderson Elementary School has 254 students. Jackson Elementary School has 362 students.

Which school has more students? Tell how you know. Use a model or number sentence to show.

14. Maya plants marigolds in 2 rows. In each row, she plants 5 marigolds.

Draw a model to match the marigold Maya plants.

How many marigolds does Maya plant?

....

15. Find the sum.

$18 + 25 + 13 =$ _____

....

16. Grace has 23 stamps in one pile. She has 27 stamps in another pile. Draw a model to show the total number of stamps, and find the total.

17. Michael's desk is 85 centimeters wide. Hamza's desk is 62 centimeters wide. What is the difference between the two lengths?

---

18. Write the standard form of 200 + 30 + 6.

---

19. Milo made a paper chain 39 inches long. Alice made a paper chain 28 inches long. Whose chain is longer? By how much?

20. Use the number line to show 42 − 5.

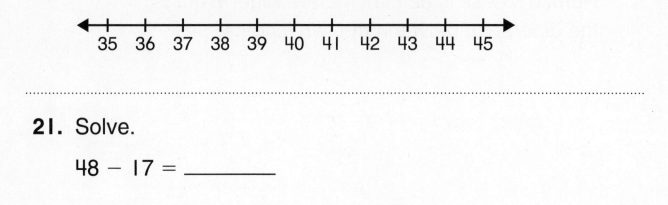

21. Solve.

48 − 17 = _____

22. Shandra walks her dog in the afternoon at the time shown on the clock.

At what time does Shandra walk her dog in the afternoon? Include A.M. or P.M.

23. Divide the circle into 4 equal parts.

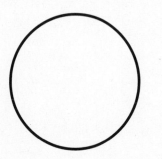

24. Use the number line to show the sum of 64 and 7.

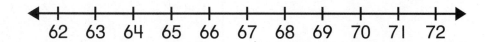

62 63 64 65 66 67 68 69 70 71 72

25. Sam counts 241 blocks. Then he uses 100 blocks for a project. How many blocks remain?

26. Anna is thinking of a shape. She says these things about the shape:

- The shape has 4 sides.

- Two of the sides have the same short length.

- The other two sides have the same long length.

- The shape is not a rectangle.

Draw Anna's shape, and write its name.

27.

a. Draw four lines across the rectangle to make five smaller rectangles, each the same size.

b. Draw four lines to divide the rectangles into squares.

c. How many squares did you make?

28. Which number is 10 fewer than 698?

(A) 688

(B) 668

(C) 708

(D) 578

29. Mr. Thomas has 48 bird feeders for sale at his store. Then he receives 55 more bird feeders. How many bird feeders does he have?

30. John arranges fruit slices in two rows, as shown below. Is there an even or odd number of slices? Tell how you know.

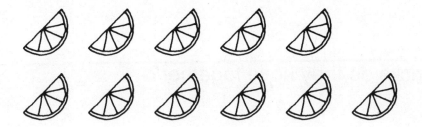

31. What is the next number in the sequence?

15, 20, 25, 30, 35, 40, _____

32. Howard has 212 bricks.

Uri adds 189 bricks.

Draw a model to show the sum.

How many bricks do they have together?

---

33. Draw a model to show this subtraction problem:

46 − 28

34. In which group does each figure belong? Write the letter of the figure in the correct box.

No equal parts	2 equal parts	4 equal parts

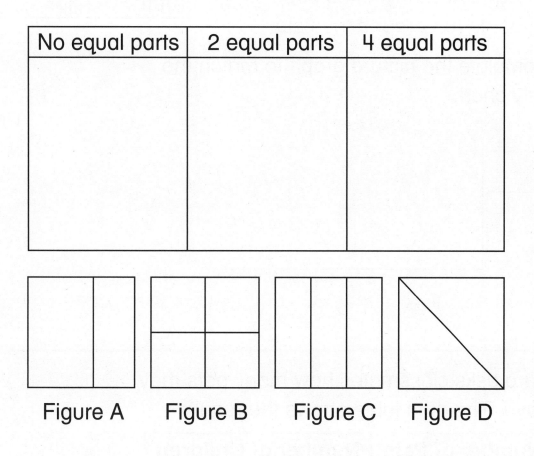

Figure A   Figure B   Figure C   Figure D

35. Divide the rectangle below into 2 equal rows and 3 equal columns. How many squares are in the rectangle?

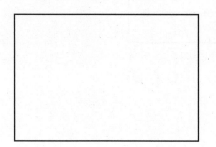

36. The students in Ms. O'Neil's class run around the field. The tally chart shows how many times three students run around the field.

Stella	|||
Marge	卌	
Jeff	卌

Complete the picture graph to match the tally chart.

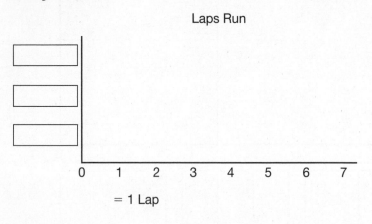

Laps Run

= 1 Lap

---

37. Sara asks classmates how many pets they have. The data table shows the results.

Number of Pets	Number of Children
0	1
1	6
2	3
3	1
4	2

Draw Xs to show Sara's data on a line plot.

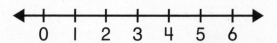

0 1 2 3 4 5 6

38. Find the sum.

$32 + 49 = \boxed{}$

---

39. Complete each inequality. Tell with words or a model how you know which number is less.

487 _____ 478   709 _____ 712

---

40. Which of these is equal to 19?
Circle Yes or No.

9 + 9	Yes	No
11 + 8	Yes	No
6 + 13	Yes	No
15 + 4	Yes	No

Performance Task 3

Part A

Jimmy and his father love football. They always go to the high school football games. Their team is the Cougars. Jimmy wants to know how many people go to the Cougars' games.

At Game 1 of the Cougars' football season, there are between 500 and 600 people at the game.

1. Write a number that could be the number of people at Game 1.

   There are _____ fans at Game 1.

2. Draw a model to show this number.

3. Write the number in expanded form.

Part B

Between 600 and 700 people come to the Cougars'
Game 2.

4. Write a number that could be the number of
people at Game 2.

There are _____ fans at Game 2.

5. Write a number sentence to compare the
number of people at Game 1 with Game 2.
Use your numbers.

6. Are there more people at Game 2 than at
Game 1? Explain how you know.

Name _____

Performance Task 4

Part A

The students in Ms. Jones' second grade class set up a bird feeder outside their classroom. Every morning they count the number of birds at the bird feeder. The table shows the number of birds that the students counted in four days.

Day	Monday	Tuesday	Wednesday	Thursday
Number of Birds	11	7	10	9

1. Angie and Willa want to display the data they collect. Angie wants to make a bar graph. Willa wants to make a pictograph. Which type of graph should they make? Tell why you think so.

2. Draw a graph, either a bar graph or a pictograph, to show the data.

Monday Tuesday Wednesday Thursday

Part B

Aldo and Emma compare the number of birds they counted.

Aldo says that they counted more birds on Monday and Tuesday combined than on Wednesday and Thursday combined.

Emma says they counted fewer birds on Monday and Tuesday combined than on Wednesday and Thursday combined.

3. Who do you agree with? Tell why. Use models or equations in your answer.

Answers and Rubrics

Page CC 1

Common Core Standards Practice

2.OA.1 Use addition and subtraction within 100 to solve one- and two-step word problems involving situations of adding to, taking from, putting together, taking apart, and comparing, with unknowns in all positions, e.g., by using drawings and equations with a symbol for the unknown number to represent the problem.

1. Samantha has 6 toy cars.
   Roger has 10 toy cars.
   How many do they have in all?

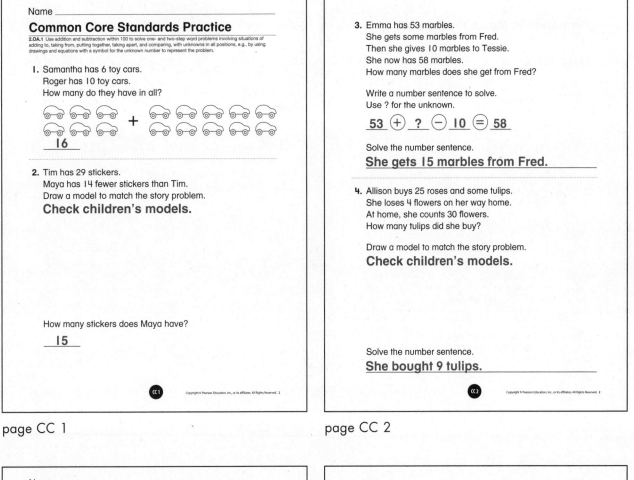

   16

2. Tim has 29 stickers.
   Maya has 14 fewer stickers than Tim.
   Draw a model to match the story problem.
   Check children's models.

   How many stickers does Maya have?
   15

Page CC 2

3. Emma has 53 marbles.
   She gets some marbles from Fred.
   Then she gives 10 marbles to Tessie.
   She now has 58 marbles.
   How many marbles does she get from Fred?

   Write a number sentence to solve.
   Use ? for the unknown.

   __53__ $+$ __?__ $-$ __10__ $=$ __58__

   Solve the number sentence.
   She gets 15 marbles from Fred.

4. Allison buys 25 roses and some tulips.
   She loses 4 flowers on her way home.
   At home, she counts 30 flowers.
   How many tulips did she buy?

   Draw a model to match the story problem.
   Check children's models.

   Solve the number sentence.
   She bought 9 tulips.

Page CC 3

Common Core Standards Practice

2.OA.2 Fluently add and subtract within 20 using mental strategies. By end of Grade 2, know from memory all sums of two one-digit numbers.

Solve.

1. $7 + 12 =$ ☐
   - Ⓐ 20
   - ● 19
   - Ⓒ 12
   - Ⓓ 15

2. $8 + 9 =$ ☐
   - Ⓐ 20
   - Ⓑ 19
   - ● 17
   - Ⓓ 15

3. $13 - 7 =$ ☐
   6

4. $13 + 6 =$ ☐
   19

5. $14 - 6 =$ ☐
   8

6. $19 - 5 =$ ☐
   14

Page CC 4

7. $18 - 9 =$ ☐
   - Ⓐ 7
   - Ⓑ 8
   - ● 9
   - Ⓓ 10

8. $12 - 9 =$ ☐
   - ● 3
   - Ⓑ 4
   - Ⓒ 5
   - Ⓓ 6

9. $15 - 6 =$ ☐
   9

10. $4 + 16 =$ ☐
    20

11. $5 + 12 =$ ☐
    17

12. $13 + 7 =$ ☐
    20

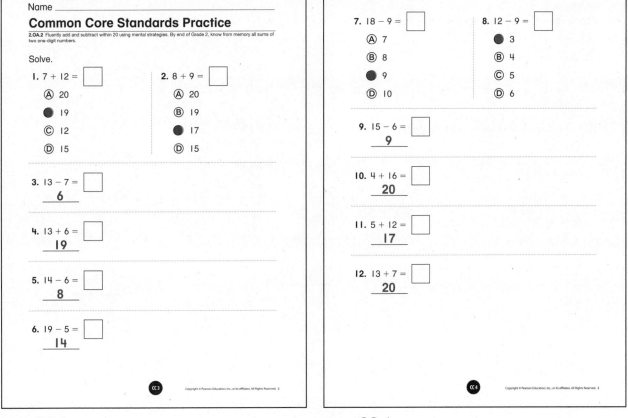

page CC 1

page CC 2

page CC 3

page CC 4

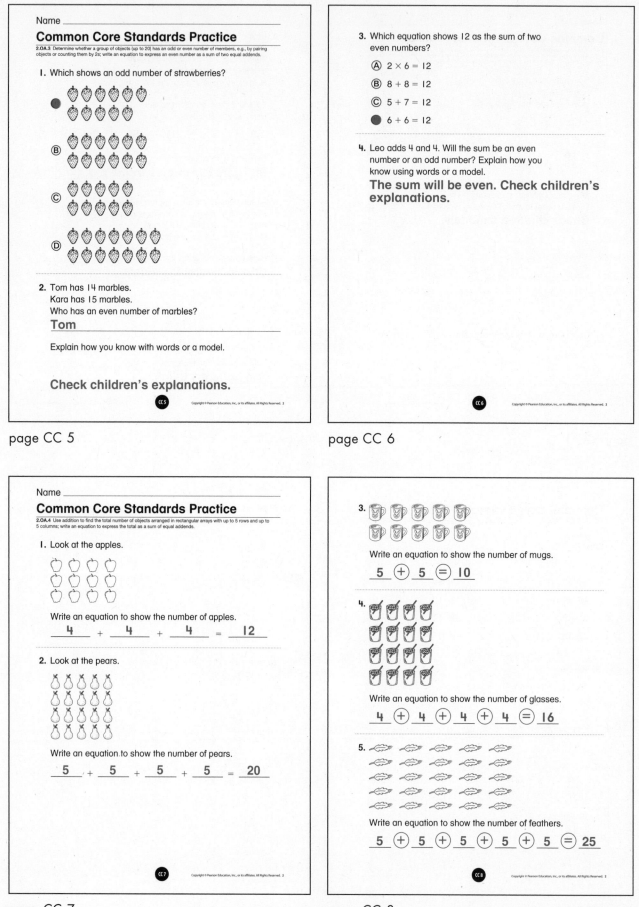

Name _____

Common Core Standards Practice

2.OA.3 Determine whether a group of objects (up to 20) has an odd or even number of members, e.g., by pairing objects or counting them by 2s; write an equation to express an even number as a sum of two equal addends.

1. Which shows an odd number of strawberries?

● A

B

C

D

2. Tom has 14 marbles.
   Kara has 15 marbles.
   Who has an even number of marbles?

   Tom

   Explain how you know with words or a model.

   Check children's explanations.

page CC 5

---

3. Which equation shows 12 as the sum of two even numbers?

   (A) $2 \times 6 = 12$

   (B) $8 + 8 = 12$

   (C) $5 + 7 = 12$

   ● $6 + 6 = 12$

4. Leo adds 4 and 4. Will the sum be an even number or an odd number? Explain how you know using words or a model.

   The sum will be even. Check children's explanations.

page CC 6

Name _____

Common Core Standards Practice

2.OA.4 Use addition to find the total number of objects arranged in rectangular arrays with up to 5 rows and up to 5 columns; write an equation to express the total as a sum of equal addends.

1. Look at the apples.

   Write an equation to show the number of apples.

   $\underline{4} + \underline{4} + \underline{4} = \underline{12}$

2. Look at the pears.

   Write an equation to show the number of pears.

   $\underline{5} + \underline{5} + \underline{5} + \underline{5} = \underline{20}$

page CC 7

3.

   Write an equation to show the number of mugs.

   $\underline{5} \oplus \underline{5} \ominus \underline{10}$

4.

   Write an equation to show the number of glasses.

   $\underline{4} \oplus \underline{4} \oplus \underline{4} \oplus \underline{4} \ominus \underline{16}$

5.

   Write an equation to show the number of feathers.

   $\underline{5} \oplus \underline{5} \oplus \underline{5} \oplus \underline{5} \oplus \underline{5} \ominus \underline{25}$

page CC 8

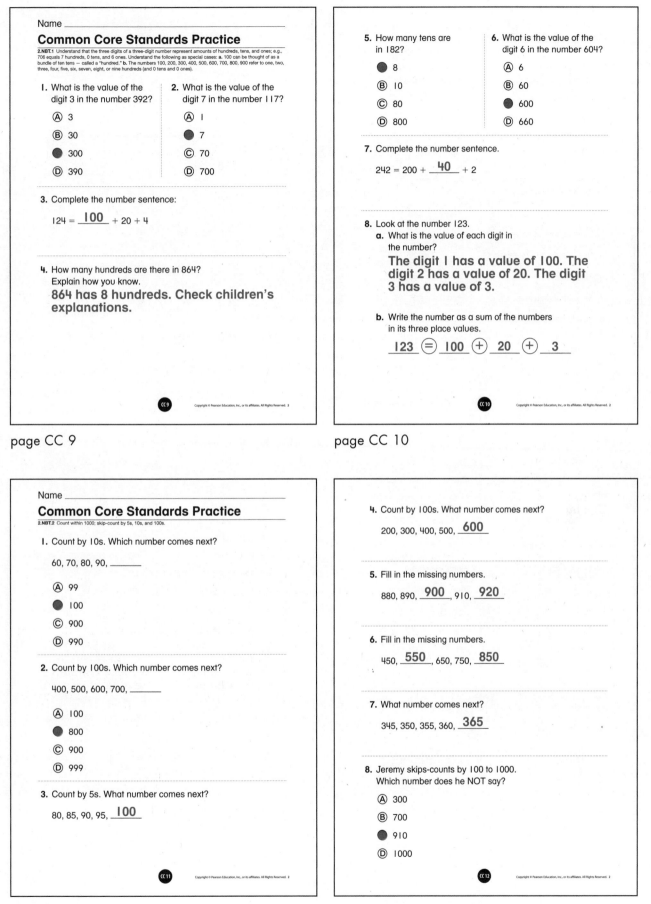

Name _____

Common Core Standards Practice

2.NBT.1 Understand that the three digits of a three-digit number represent amounts of hundreds, tens, and ones; e.g., 706 equals 7 hundreds, 0 tens, and 6 ones. Understand the following as special cases: **a.** 100 can be thought of as a bundle of ten tens — called a "hundred." **b.** The numbers 100, 200, 300, 400, 500, 600, 700, 800, 900 refer to one, two, three, four, five, six, seven, eight, or nine hundreds (and 0 tens and 0 ones).

1. What is the value of the digit 3 in the number 392?

Ⓐ 3
Ⓑ 30
● 300
Ⓓ 390

2. What is the value of the digit 7 in the number 117?

Ⓐ 1
● 7
Ⓒ 70
Ⓓ 700

3. Complete the number sentence:

124 = __100__ + 20 + 4

4. How many hundreds are there in 864? Explain how you know.

864 has 8 hundreds. Check children's explanations.

page CC 9

---

5. How many tens are in 182?

● 8
Ⓑ 10
Ⓒ 80
Ⓓ 800

6. What is the value of the digit 6 in the number 604?

Ⓐ 6
Ⓑ 60
● 600
Ⓓ 660

7. Complete the number sentence.

242 = 200 + __40__ + 2

8. Look at the number 123.

a. What is the value of each digit in the number?

The digit 1 has a value of 100. The digit 2 has a value of 20. The digit 3 has a value of 3.

b. Write the number as a sum of the numbers in its three place values.

__123__ Ⓔ __100__ ⊕ __20__ ⊕ __3__

page CC 10

Name _____

Common Core Standards Practice

2.NBT.2 Count within 1000; skip-count by 5s, 10s, and 100s.

1. Count by 10s. Which number comes next?

60, 70, 80, 90, _____

Ⓐ 99
● 100
Ⓒ 900
Ⓓ 990

2. Count by 100s. Which number comes next?

400, 500, 600, 700, _____

Ⓐ 100
● 800
Ⓒ 900
Ⓓ 999

3. Count by 5s. What number comes next?

80, 85, 90, 95, __100__

page CC 11

---

4. Count by 100s. What number comes next?

200, 300, 400, 500, __600__

5. Fill in the missing numbers.

880, 890, __900__, 910, __920__

6. Fill in the missing numbers.

450, __550__, 650, 750, __850__

7. What number comes next?

345, 350, 355, 360, __365__

8. Jeremy skips-counts by 100 to 1000. Which number does he NOT say?

Ⓐ 300
Ⓑ 700
● 910
Ⓓ 1000

page CC 12

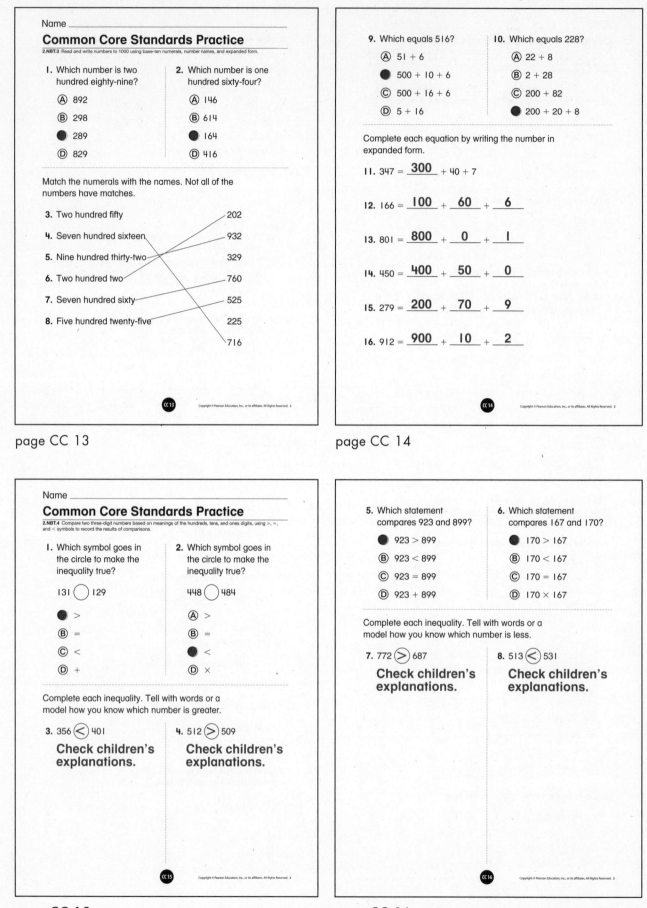

page CC 13

Name _____

Common Core Standards Practice
2.NBT.3 Read and write numbers to 1000 using base-ten numerals, number names, and expanded form.

1. Which number is two hundred eighty-nine?
- (A) 892
- (B) 298
- ● 289
- (D) 829

2. Which number is one hundred sixty-four?
- (A) 146
- (B) 614
- ● 164
- (D) 416

Match the numerals with the names. Not all of the numbers have matches.

3. Two hundred fifty   202
4. Seven hundred sixteen   932
5. Nine hundred thirty-two   329
6. Two hundred two   760
7. Seven hundred sixty   525
8. Five hundred twenty-five 225
                                 716

page CC 14

9. Which equals 516?
- (A) 51 + 6
- ● 500 + 10 + 6
- (C) 500 + 16 + 6
- (D) 5 + 16

10. Which equals 228?
- (A) 22 + 8
- (B) 2 + 28
- (C) 200 + 82
- ● 200 + 20 + 8

Complete each equation by writing the number in expanded form.

11. 347 = __300__ + 40 + 7

12. 166 = __100__ + __60__ + __6__

13. 801 = __800__ + __0__ + __1__

14. 450 = __400__ + __50__ + __0__

15. 279 = __200__ + __70__ + __9__

16. 912 = __900__ + __10__ + __2__

page CC 15

Name _____

Common Core Standards Practice
2.NBT.4 Compare two three-digit numbers based on meanings of the hundreds, tens, and ones digits, using >, =, and < symbols to record the results of comparisons.

1. Which symbol goes in the circle to make the inequality true?

131 ◯ 129
- ● >
- (B) =
- (C) <
- (D) +

2. Which symbol goes in the circle to make the inequality true?

448 ◯ 484
- (A) >
- (B) =
- ● <
- (D) ×

Complete each inequality. Tell with words or a model how you know which number is greater.

3. 356 (<) 401

Check children's explanations.

4. 512 (>) 509

Check children's explanations.

page CC 16

5. Which statement compares 923 and 899?
- ● 923 > 899
- (B) 923 < 899
- (C) 923 = 899
- (D) 923 + 899

6. Which statement compares 167 and 170?
- ● 170 > 167
- (B) 170 < 167
- (C) 170 = 167
- (D) 170 × 167

Complete each inequality. Tell with words or a model how you know which number is less.

7. 772 (>) 687

Check children's explanations.

8. 513 (<) 531

Check children's explanations.

T4

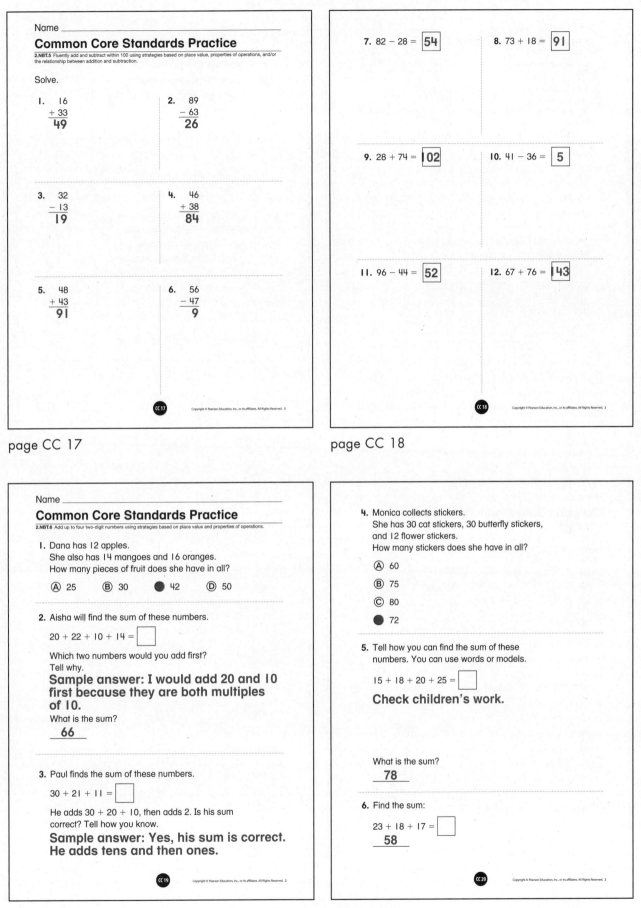

page CC 17

page CC 18

page CC 19

page CC 20

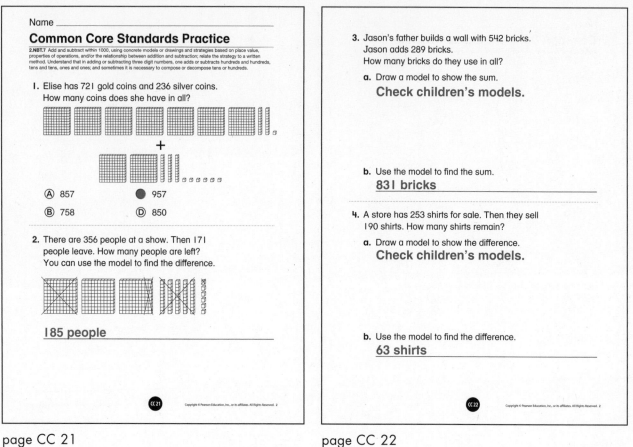

Page CC 21

Common Core Standards Practice

2.NBT.7 Add and subtract within 1000, using concrete models or drawings and strategies based on place value, properties of operations, and/or the relationship between addition and subtraction; relate the strategy to a written method. Understand that in adding or subtracting three digit numbers, one adds or subtracts hundreds and hundreds, tens and tens, ones and ones; and sometimes it is necessary to compose or decompose tens or hundreds.

1. Elise has 721 gold coins and 236 silver coins. How many coins does she have in all?

   (A) 857   ● 957

   (B) 758   (D) 850

2. There are 356 people at a show. Then 171 people leave. How many people are left? You can use the model to find the difference.

   185 people

Copyright © Pearson Education, Inc., or its affiliates. All Rights Reserved. 2

page CC 21

Page CC 22

3. Jason's father builds a wall with 542 bricks. Jason adds 289 bricks. How many bricks do they use in all?

   a. Draw a model to show the sum.
   Check children's models.

   b. Use the model to find the sum.
   831 bricks

4. A store has 253 shirts for sale. Then they sell 190 shirts. How many shirts remain?

   a. Draw a model to show the difference.
   Check children's models.

   b. Use the model to find the difference.
   63 shirts

Copyright © Pearson Education, Inc., or its affiliates. All Rights Reserved. 2

page CC 22

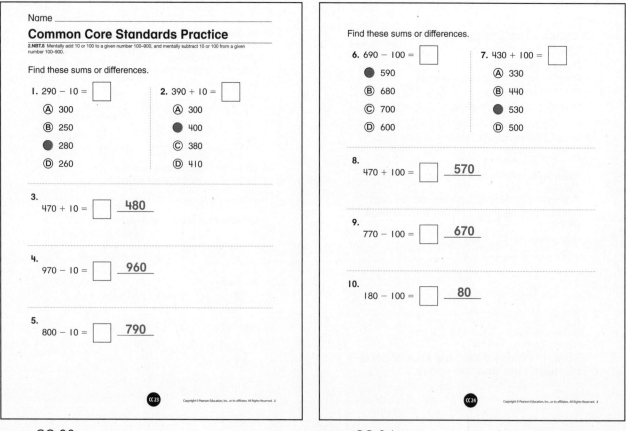

Page CC 23

Common Core Standards Practice

2.NBT.8 Mentally add 10 or 100 to a given number 100–900, and mentally subtract 10 or 100 from a given number 100–900.

Find these sums or differences.

1. $290 - 10 =$ ☐

   (A) 300

   (B) 250

   ● 280

   (D) 260

2. $390 + 10 =$ ☐

   (A) 300

   ● 400

   (C) 380

   (D) 410

3. $470 + 10 =$ ☐ __480__

4. $970 - 10 =$ ☐ __960__

5. $800 - 10 =$ ☐ __790__

Copyright © Pearson Education, Inc., or its affiliates. All Rights Reserved. 2

page CC 23

Page CC 24

Find these sums or differences.

6. $690 - 100 =$ ☐

   ● 590

   (B) 680

   (C) 700

   (D) 600

7. $430 + 100 =$ ☐

   (A) 330

   (B) 440

   ● 530

   (D) 500

8. $470 + 100 =$ ☐ __570__

9. $770 - 100 =$ ☐ __670__

10. $180 - 100 =$ ☐ __80__

Copyright © Pearson Education, Inc., or its affiliates. All Rights Reserved. 2

page CC 24

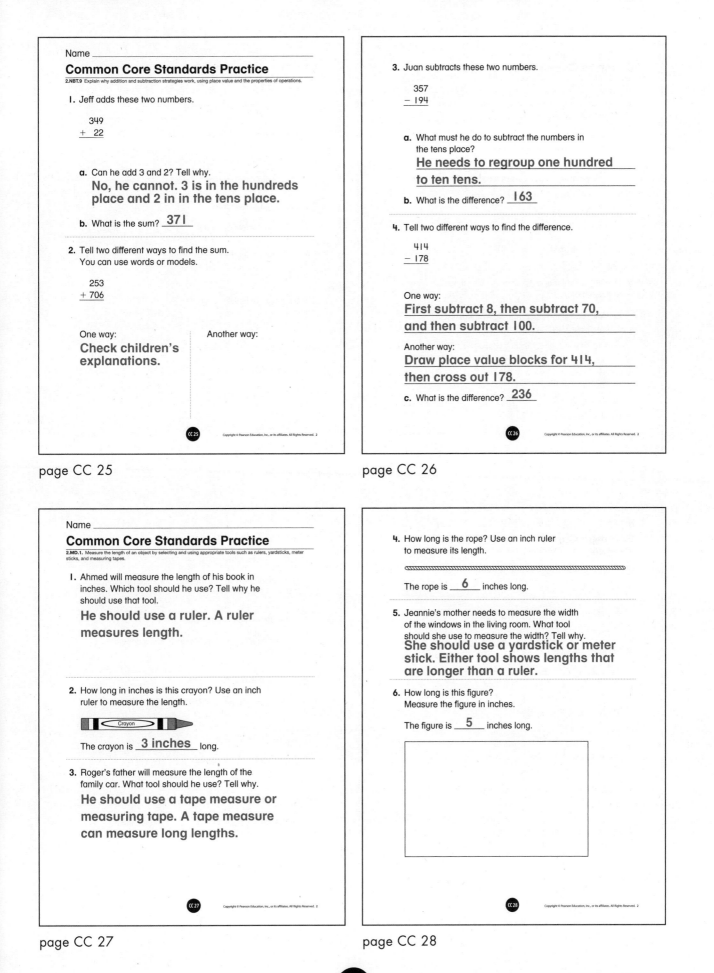

page CC 25

Name _____

Common Core Standards Practice

2.NBT.9 Explain why addition and subtraction strategies work, using place value and the properties of operations.

1. Jeff adds these two numbers.

   349
   + 22

   a. Can he add 3 and 2? Tell why.
   No, he cannot. 3 is in the hundreds place and 2 in in the tens place.

   b. What is the sum? **371**

2. Tell two different ways to find the sum.
   You can use words or models.

   253
   + 706

   One way: Another way:
   Check children's
   explanations.

page CC 26

3. Juan subtracts these two numbers.

   357
   − 194

   a. What must he do to subtract the numbers in the tens place?
   He needs to regroup one hundred to ten tens.

   b. What is the difference? **163**

4. Tell two different ways to find the difference.

   414
   − 178

   One way:
   First subtract 8, then subtract 70, and then subtract 100.

   Another way:
   Draw place value blocks for 414, then cross out 178.

   c. What is the difference? **236**

page CC 27

Name _____

Common Core Standards Practice

2.MD.1. Measure the length of an object by selecting and using appropriate tools such as rulers, yardsticks, meter sticks, and measuring tapes.

1. Ahmed will measure the length of his book in inches. Which tool should he use? Tell why he should use that tool.
   He should use a ruler. A ruler measures length.

2. How long in inches is this crayon? Use an inch ruler to measure the length.

   The crayon is **3 inches** long.

3. Roger's father will measure the length of the family car. What tool should he use? Tell why.
   He should use a tape measure or measuring tape. A tape measure can measure long lengths.

page CC 28

4. How long is the rope? Use an inch ruler to measure its length.

   The rope is **6** inches long.

5. Jeannie's mother needs to measure the width of the windows in the living room. What tool should she use to measure the width? Tell why.
   She should use a yardstick or meter stick. Either tool shows lengths that are longer than a ruler.

6. How long is this figure?
   Measure the figure in inches.

   The figure is **5** inches long.

Name _____

Common Core Standards Practice

2.MD.2 Measure the length of an object twice, using length units of different lengths for the two measurements; describe how the two measurements relate to the size of the unit chosen.

Check measurements for accuracy.

1. Use a centimeter straight edge or meter stick to make these measurements.

   a. How wide is one window in the classroom? Measure in centimeters. Then measure in meters.

   The window is _____ centimeters wide.

   The window is _____ meters wide.

   b. Which measurement is greater?
   measurement in centimeters

   c. Which unit is larger? **a meter**

2. Use an inch ruler or a yardstick to make these measurements.

   a. How wide is the classroom door? Measure in inches. Then measure in feet.

   The door is _____ inches wide.

   The door is _____ feet wide.

   b. Which measurement is greater?
   the measurement in inches

   c. Which unit is larger? **a foot**

CC 29   Copyright © Pearson Education, Inc., or its affiliates. All Rights Reserved. 2

page CC 29

The children in Mrs. Peters' class made measurements in their classroom. Circle the most likely unit for each measurement.

3. the width of the chalkboard

   2 (centimeters, **meters**)

4. the length of a crayon

   10 (**centimeters**, meters)

5. the height of the room

   220 (**centimeters**, meters)

6. the length of a pencil

   5 (**inches**, feet)

7. the height of a child

   3 (inches, **feet**)

8. the width of a computer screen

   15 (**inches**, feet)

CC 30   Copyright © Pearson Education, Inc., or its affiliates. All Rights Reserved. 2

page CC 30

Name _____

Common Core Standards Practice

2.MD.3 Estimate lengths using units of inches, feet, centimeters, and meters.

Circle the best estimate for these lengths.

1. the height of a chair

   3 inches   10 inches   **25 inches**

2. the length of a crayon

   4 inches   12 inches   32 inches

3. the width of a child's desk

   2 inches   **20 inches**   200 inches

4. the length of a school bus

   2 feet   **38 feet**   380 feet

5. the height of a house with 2 floors

   3 feet   10 feet   **30 feet**

CC 31   Copyright © Pearson Education, Inc., or its affiliates. All Rights Reserved. 2

page CC 31

Circle the best estimate for these lengths.

6. the width of a chair

   4 centimeters   **40 centimeters**   400 centimeters

7. the width of a bracelet

   1 centimeter   7 centimeters   30 centimeters

8. the height of a bottle of juice

   14 centimeters   60 centimeters   100 centimeters

9. the height of an adult

   2 meters   10 meters   20 meters

10. the length of a driveway to a house

    2 meters   **15 meters**   600 meters

CC 32   Copyright © Pearson Education, Inc., or its affiliates. All Rights Reserved. 2

page CC 32

T8

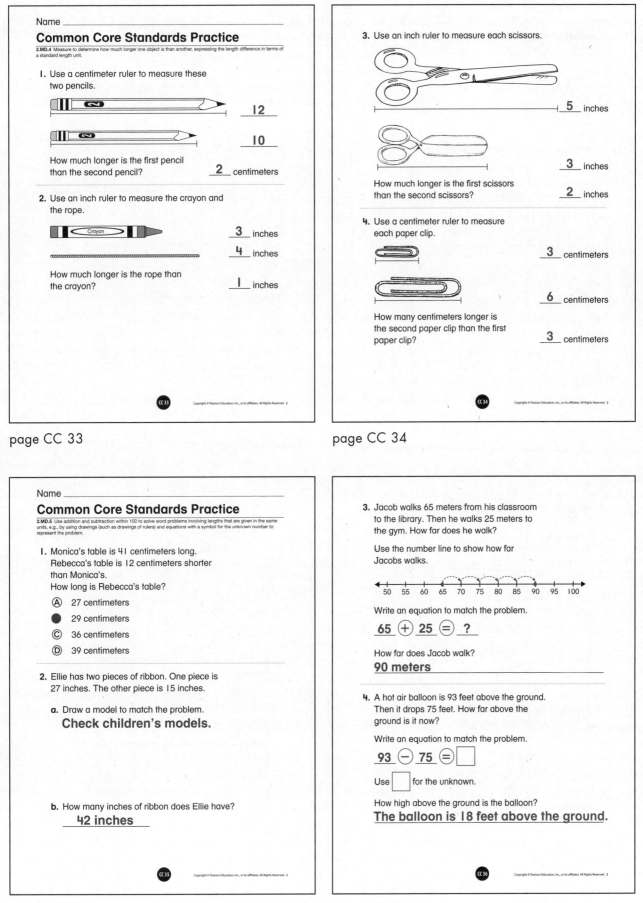

page CC 33

Name _____

Common Core Standards Practice

2.MD.4 Measure to determine how much longer one object is than another, expressing the length difference in terms of a standard length unit.

1. Use a centimeter ruler to measure these two pencils.

   ___12___

   ___10___

   How much longer is the first pencil than the second pencil? ___2___ centimeters

2. Use an inch ruler to measure the crayon and the rope.

   Crayon ___3___ inches

   ___4___ inches

   How much longer is the rope than the crayon? ___1___ inches

---

page CC 34

3. Use an inch ruler to measure each scissors.

   ___5___ inches

   ___3___ inches

   How much longer is the first scissors than the second scissors? ___2___ inches

4. Use a centimeter ruler to measure each paper clip.

   ___3___ centimeters

   ___6___ centimeters

   How many centimeters longer is the second paper clip than the first paper clip? ___3___ centimeters

---

page CC 35

Name _____

Common Core Standards Practice

2.MD.5 Use addition and subtraction within 100 to solve word problems involving lengths that are given in the same units, e.g., by using drawings (such as drawings of rulers) and equations with a symbol for the unknown number to represent the problem.

1. Monica's table is 41 centimeters long. Rebecca's table is 12 centimeters shorter than Monica's. How long is Rebecca's table?

   Ⓐ 27 centimeters

   ● 29 centimeters

   Ⓒ 36 centimeters

   Ⓓ 39 centimeters

2. Ellie has two pieces of ribbon. One piece is 27 inches. The other piece is 15 inches.

   a. Draw a model to match the problem.
   Check children's models.

   b. How many inches of ribbon does Ellie have?
   42 inches

---

page CC 36

3. Jacob walks 65 meters from his classroom to the library. Then he walks 25 meters to the gym. How far does he walk?

   Use the number line to show how far Jacobs walks.

   50 55 60 65 70 75 80 85 90 95 100

   Write an equation to match the problem.

   ___65___ ⊕ ___25___ ⊜ ___?___

   How far does Jacob walk?
   90 meters

4. A hot air balloon is 93 feet above the ground. Then it drops 75 feet. How far above the ground is it now?

   Write an equation to match the problem.

   ___93___ ⊖ ___75___ ⊜ ☐

   Use ☐ for the unknown.

   How high above the ground is the balloon?
   The balloon is 18 feet above the ground.

Name _____

Common Core Standards Practice

2.MD.6 Represent whole numbers as lengths from 0 on a number line diagram with equally spaced points corresponding to the numbers 0, 1, 2, ..., and represent whole-number sums and differences within 100 on a number line diagram.

1. Pencil A is 3 inches long.
   Pencil B is 5 inches long.
   Pencil C is 8 inches long.
   Write A, B, and C on the number line to show each length.

   A   B   C
   ◄─┼─┼─┼─┼─┼─┼─┼─┼─┼─┼─►
     0 1 2 3 4 5 6 7 8 9 10

2. Use the number line below to represent this addition number sentence.

   45 + 6 = ☐

   ◄─┼─┼─┼─┼─┼─┼─┼─┼─┼─┼─►
     45 46 47 48 49 50 51 52 53 54 55

CC 37

Use the number line to represent these number sentences.

3. 42 − 6

   ◄─┼─┼─┼─┼─┼─┼─┼─┼─┼─┼─►
     35 36 37 38 39 40 41 42 43 44 45

4. 58 − 9

   ◄─┼─┼─┼─┼─┼─┼─┼─┼─┼─┼─►
     48 49 50 51 52 53 54 55 56 57 58

5. 81 − 7

   ◄─┼─┼─┼─┼─┼─┼─┼─┼─┼─┼─►
     71 72 73 74 75 76 77 78 79 80 81

6. 25 + 25

   ◄─┼─┼─┼─┼─┼─┼─┼─┼─┼─┼─►
     25 30 35 40 45 50 55 60 65 70 75

7. 70 − 15

   ◄─┼─┼─┼─┼─┼─┼─┼─┼─┼─┼─►
     25 30 35 40 45 50 55 60 65 70 75

8. 85 − 30

   ◄─┼─┼─┼─┼─┼─┼─┼─┼─┼─┼─►
     35 40 45 50 55 60 65 70 75 80 85

CC 38

Name _____

Common Core Standards Practice

2.MD.7 Tell and write time from analog and digital clocks to the nearest five minutes, using a.m. and p.m.

1. The clock shows the time that Joel's father wakes up every morning.

   What time does Joel's father wake up?
   Use A.M. or P.M.

   __5__ : __35__ A.M.

2. Sadie gets home from school every afternoon at the time shown on the clock below.

   What time does Sadie get home from school?
   Use A.M. or P.M.

   __3__ : __45__ P.M.

CC 39

---

3. Math class begins after lunch.
   The clock shows the time.

   What time does math class begin?
   Use A.M. or P.M.

   __1__ : __30__ P.M.

4. Mr. Jenkins comes home late one evening.
   The clock shows the time.

   What time does Mr. Jenkins come home?
   Use A.M. or P.M.

   __8__ : __20__ P.M.

CC 40

page CC 37

page CC 38

page CC 39

page CC 40

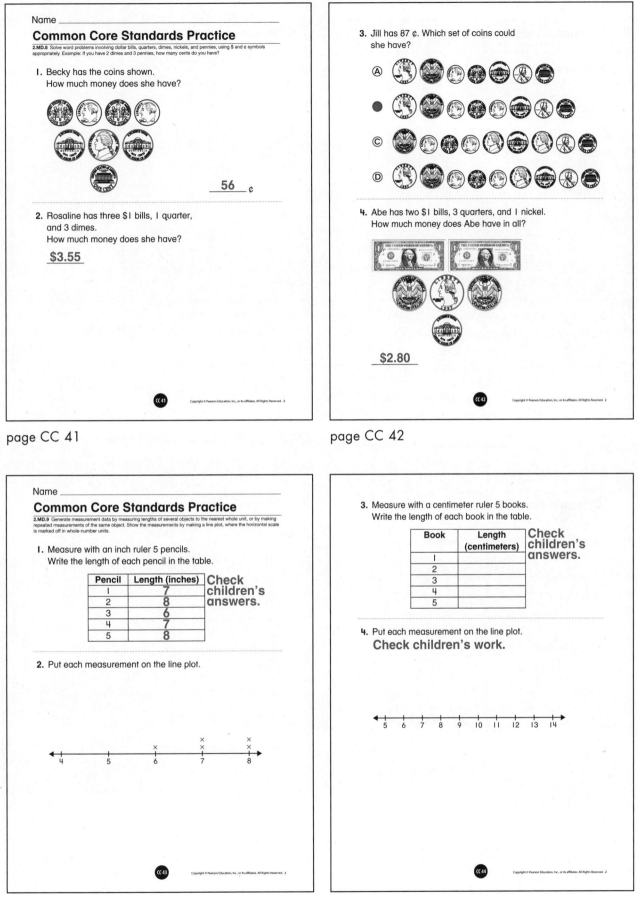

page CC 41

page CC 42

page CC 43

page CC 44

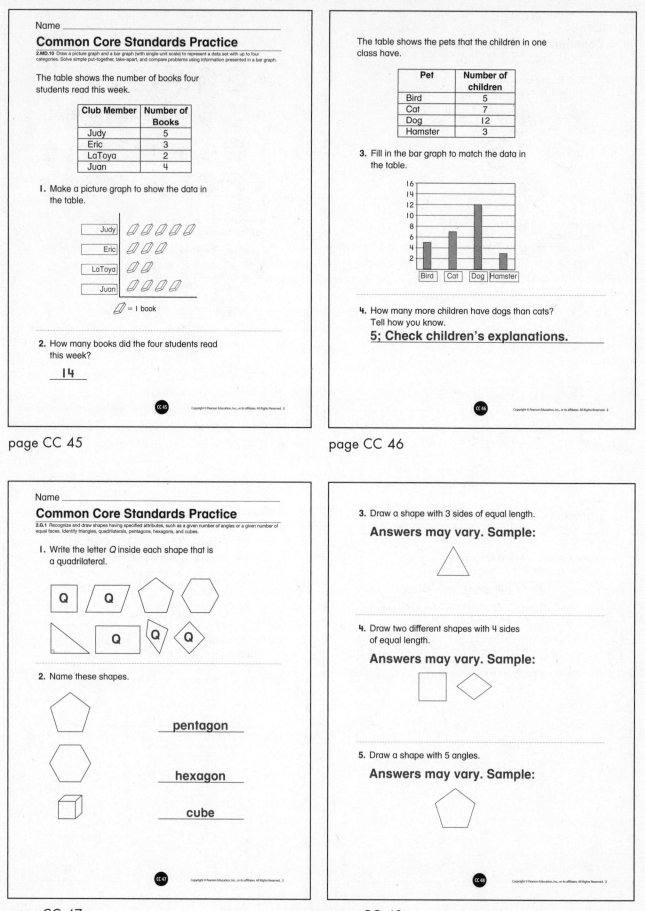

page CC 45

Name _____

Common Core Standards Practice

2.MD.10 Draw a picture graph and a bar graph (with single-unit scale) to represent a data set with up to four categories. Solve simple put-together, take-apart, and compare problems using information presented in a bar graph.

The table shows the number of books four students read this week.

Club Member	Number of Books
Judy	5
Eric	3
LaToya	2
Juan	4

1. Make a picture graph to show the data in the table.

Judy	▱▱▱▱▱
Eric	▱▱▱
LaToya	▱▱
Juan	▱▱▱▱

▱ = 1 book

2. How many books did the four students read this week?

__14__

---

page CC 46

The table shows the pets that the children in one class have.

Pet	Number of children
Bird	5
Cat	7
Dog	12
Hamster	3

3. Fill in the bar graph to match the data in the table.

4. How many more children have dogs than cats? Tell how you know.

5; Check children's explanations.

---

page CC 47

Name _____

Common Core Standards Practice

2.G.1 Recognize and draw shapes having specified attributes, such as a given number of angles or a given number of equal faces. Identify triangles, quadrilaterals, pentagons, hexagons, and cubes.

1. Write the letter *Q* inside each shape that is a quadrilateral.

2. Name these shapes.

pentagon

hexagon

cube

---

page CC 48

3. Draw a shape with 3 sides of equal length.

Answers may vary. Sample:

4. Draw two different shapes with 4 sides of equal length.

Answers may vary. Sample:

5. Draw a shape with 5 angles.

Answers may vary. Sample:

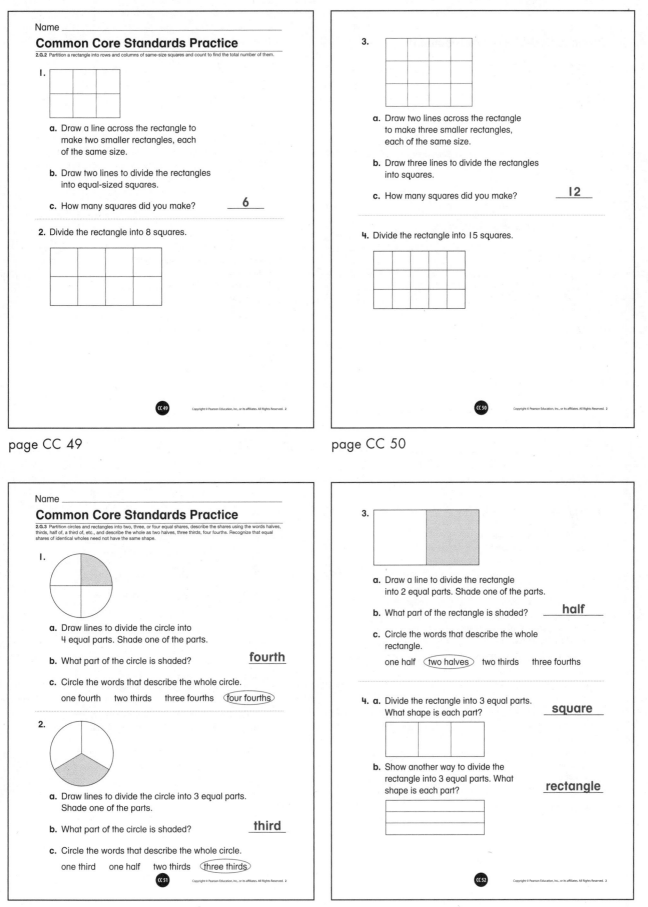

page CC 49

Name _____

Common Core Standards Practice

2.G.2 Partition a rectangle into rows and columns of same-size squares and count to find the total number of them.

1.

a. Draw a line across the rectangle to make two smaller rectangles, each of the same size.

b. Draw two lines to divide the rectangles into equal-sized squares.

c. How many squares did you make? ____6____

2. Divide the rectangle into 8 squares.

page CC 50

3.

a. Draw two lines across the rectangle to make three smaller rectangles, each of the same size.

b. Draw three lines to divide the rectangles into squares.

c. How many squares did you make? ____12____

4. Divide the rectangle into 15 squares.

page CC 51

Name _____

Common Core Standards Practice

2.G.3 Partition circles and rectangles into two, three, or four equal shares, describe the shares using the words halves, thirds, half of, a third of, etc., and describe the whole as two halves, three thirds, four fourths. Recognize that equal shares of identical wholes need not have the same shape.

1.

a. Draw lines to divide the circle into 4 equal parts. Shade one of the parts.

b. What part of the circle is shaded? **fourth**

c. Circle the words that describe the whole circle.

one fourth   two thirds   three fourths   (four fourths)

2.

a. Draw lines to divide the circle into 3 equal parts. Shade one of the parts.

b. What part of the circle is shaded? **third**

c. Circle the words that describe the whole circle.

one third   one half   two thirds   (three thirds)

page CC 52

3.

a. Draw a line to divide the rectangle into 2 equal parts. Shade one of the parts.

b. What part of the rectangle is shaded? **half**

c. Circle the words that describe the whole rectangle.

one half   (two halves)   two thirds   three fourths

4. a. Divide the rectangle into 3 equal parts. What shape is each part? **square**

b. Show another way to divide the rectangle into 3 equal parts. What shape is each part? **rectangle**

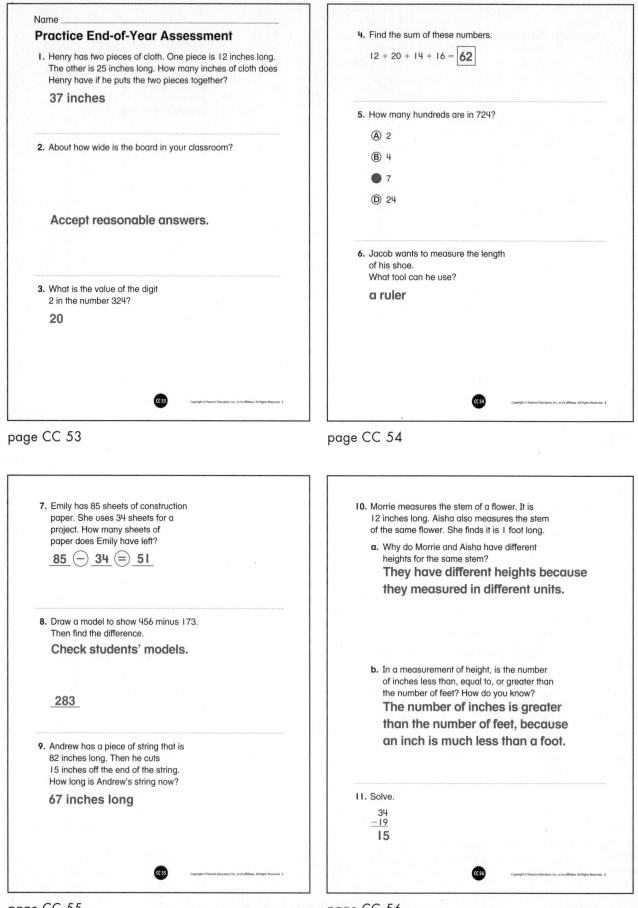

Name _____

Practice End-of-Year Assessment

1. Henry has two pieces of cloth. One piece is 12 inches long. The other is 25 inches long. How many inches of cloth does Henry have if he puts the two pieces together?

   37 inches

2. About how wide is the board in your classroom?

   Accept reasonable answers.

3. What is the value of the digit 2 in the number 324?

   20

page CC 53

4. Find the sum of these numbers.

   $12 + 20 + 14 + 16 =$ **62**

5. How many hundreds are in 724?

   Ⓐ 2

   Ⓑ 4

   ● 7

   Ⓓ 24

6. Jacob wants to measure the length of his shoe. What tool can he use?

   a ruler

page CC 54

7. Emily has 85 sheets of construction paper. She uses 34 sheets for a project. How many sheets of paper does Emily have left?

   85 ⊖ 34 ⊜ 51

8. Draw a model to show 456 minus 173. Then find the difference.

   Check students' models.

   283

9. Andrew has a piece of string that is 82 inches long. Then he cuts 15 inches off the end of the string. How long is Andrew's string now?

   67 inches long

page CC 55

10. Morrie measures the stem of a flower. It is 12 inches long. Aisha also measures the stem of the same flower. She finds it is 1 foot long.

    a. Why do Morrie and Aisha have different heights for the same stem?

    They have different heights because they measured in different units.

    b. In a measurement of height, is the number of inches less than, equal to, or greater than the number of feet? How do you know?

    The number of inches is greater than the number of feet, because an inch is much less than a foot.

11. Solve.

    $$\begin{array}{r} 34 \\ -19 \\ \hline 15 \end{array}$$

page CC 56

12. Andrew has the coins shown below.

How much money, in cents, does
he have in all?

93 cents

13. Julia read 510 pages. Jack read 479 pages.

Who read more pages? Tell how you know. Use a model
or a number sentence to show.

Julia; Check children's models.

page CC 57

---

14. A teacher arranges desks into 4 rows of 3.

Draw a model to match the desks.
Check children's models.

How many desks are there?

12

15. Find the sum.

$32 + 47 + 54 = \boxed{133}$

16. Mark has 42 marbles in one pile. He
has 16 marbles in another pile. Draw a model
to show the total number of marbles, and
find the total.

58 marbles. Check children's models.

page CC 58

---

17. Lucy's ribbon is 24 centimeters long.
Sarah's ribbon is 18 centimeters long.
How much longer is Lucy's ribbon?

6 cm

18. Write the number 751 in expanded form.

__700__ $\oplus$ __50__ $\oplus$ __1__

19. Clare made a block tower 32 inches tall.
Eric made a block tower 23 inches tall.
How many inches taller is Clare's tower?

9 inches

page CC 59

---

20. Use the number line to show 23 − 6.

21. Solve.

$94 - 78 = \boxed{16}$

22. Myron wakes up in the morning at the time
shown on the clock.

What time does Myron wake up?
Include A.M. or P.M.

6:20 A.M.

23. Divide the circle into 3 equal parts.

page CC 60

24. Use the number line to show the sum of 43 and 8.

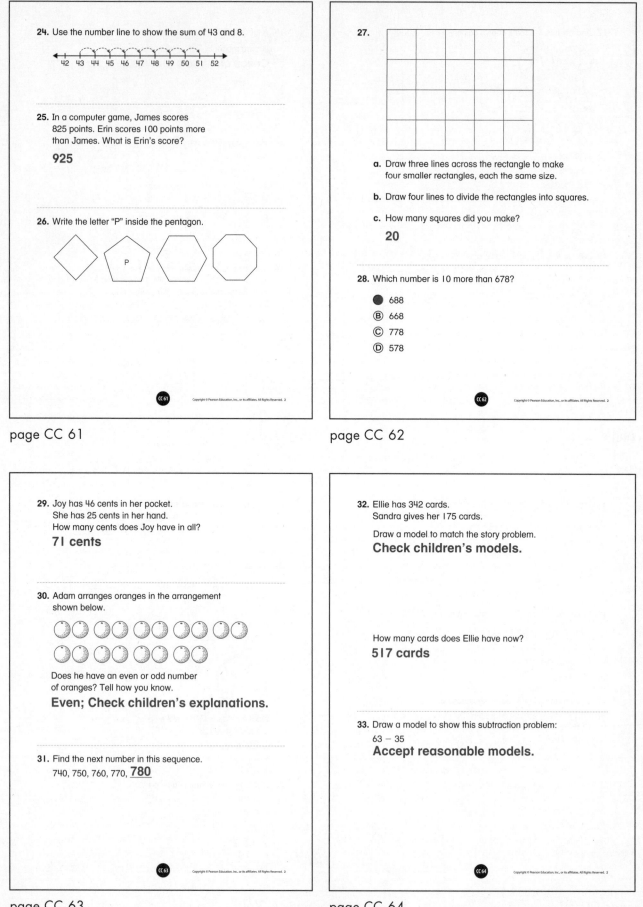

25. In a computer game, James scores 825 points. Erin scores 100 points more than James. What is Erin's score?

925

26. Write the letter "P" inside the pentagon.

page CC 61

27.

a. Draw three lines across the rectangle to make four smaller rectangles, each the same size.

b. Draw four lines to divide the rectangles into squares.

c. How many squares did you make?

20

28. Which number is 10 more than 678?

● 688

Ⓑ 668

Ⓒ 778

Ⓓ 578

page CC 62

29. Joy has 46 cents in her pocket. She has 25 cents in her hand. How many cents does Joy have in all?

71 cents

30. Adam arranges oranges in the arrangement shown below.

Does he have an even or odd number of oranges? Tell how you know.

Even; Check children's explanations.

31. Find the next number in this sequence. 740, 750, 760, 770, **780**

page CC 63

32. Ellie has 342 cards. Sandra gives her 175 cards.

Draw a model to match the story problem.

Check children's models.

How many cards does Ellie have now?

517 cards

33. Draw a model to show this subtraction problem: 63 − 35

Accept reasonable models.

page CC 64

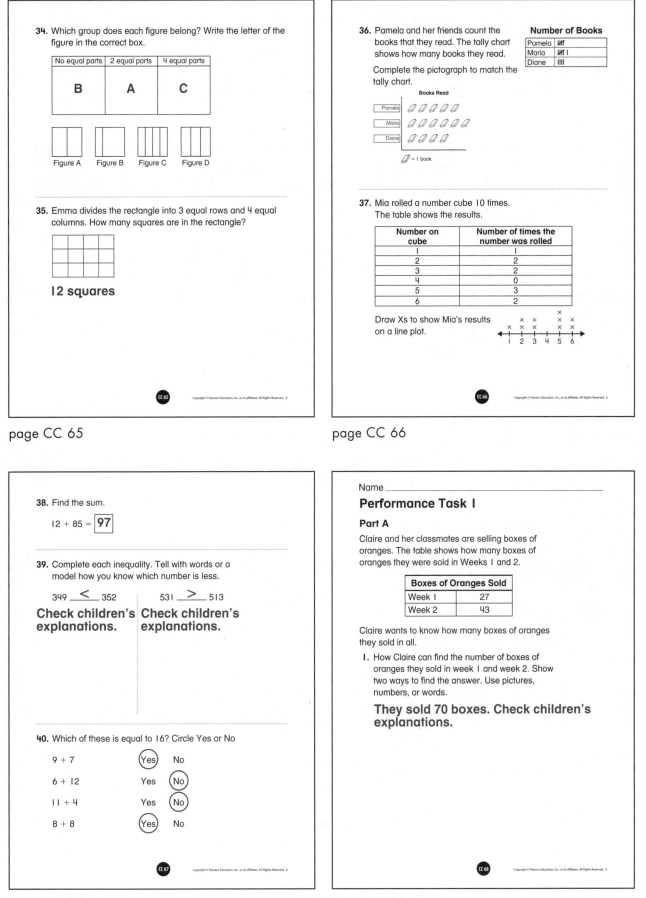

34. Which group does each figure belong? Write the letter of the figure in the correct box.

No equal parts	2 equal parts	4 equal parts
B	A	C

Figure A   Figure B   Figure C   Figure D

35. Emma divides the rectangle into 3 equal rows and 4 equal columns. How many squares are in the rectangle?

12 squares

page CC 65

36. Pamela and her friends count the books that they read. The tally chart shows how many books they read.

Number of Books

Pamela	ЖІ
Maria	ЖІ I
Diane	IIII

Complete the pictograph to match the tally chart.

Books Read

Pamela
Maria
Diane

⊘ = 1 book

37. Mia rolled a number cube 10 times. The table shows the results.

Number on cube	Number of times the number was rolled
1	1
2	2
3	2
4	0
5	3
6	2

Draw Xs to show Mia's results on a line plot.

page CC 66

38. Find the sum.

$12 + 85 = \boxed{97}$

39. Complete each inequality. Tell with words or a model how you know which number is less.

349 __<__ 352   531 __>__ 513

Check children's explanations.   **Check children's explanations.**

40. Which of these is equal to 16? Circle Yes or No

9 + 7   (Yes)   No
6 + 12   Yes   (No)
11 + 4   Yes   (No)
8 + 8   (Yes)   No

page CC 67

Name _____

Performance Task 1

Part A

Claire and her classmates are selling boxes of oranges. The table shows how many boxes of oranges they were sold in Weeks 1 and 2.

Boxes of Oranges Sold	
Week 1	27
Week 2	43

Claire wants to know how many boxes of oranges they sold in all.

1. How Claire can find the number of boxes of oranges they sold in week 1 and week 2. Show two ways to find the answer. Use pictures, numbers, or words.

They sold 70 boxes. Check children's explanations.

page CC 68

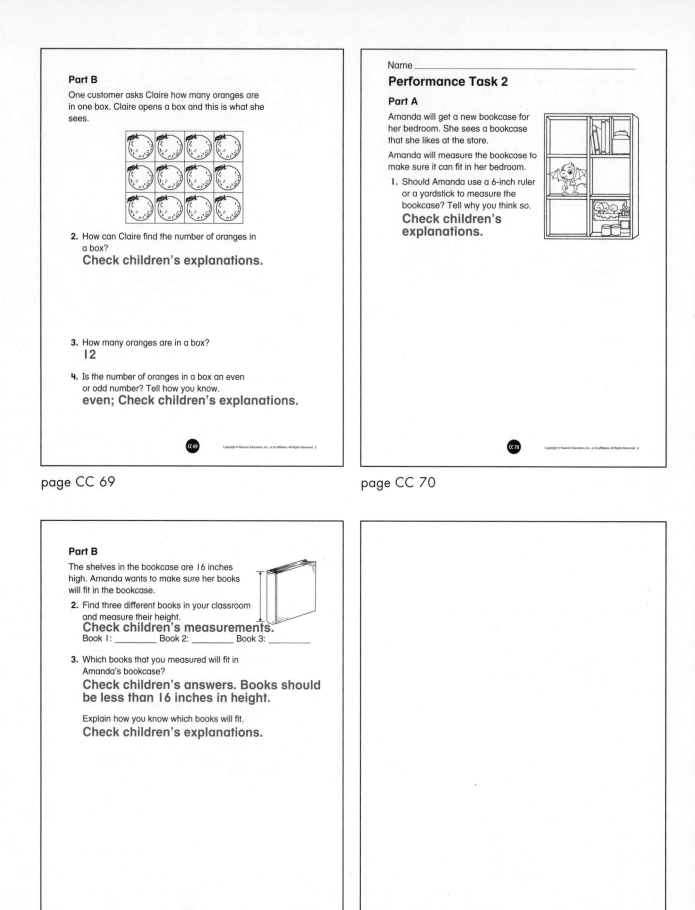

Part B

One customer asks Claire how many oranges are in one box. Claire opens a box and this is what she sees.

2. How can Claire find the number of oranges in a box?
Check children's explanations.

3. How many oranges are in a box?
12

4. Is the number of oranges in a box an even or odd number? Tell how you know.
even; Check children's explanations.

page CC 69

Performance Task 2

Part A

Amanda will get a new bookcase for her bedroom. She sees a bookcase that she likes at the store.

Amanda will measure the bookcase to make sure it can fit in her bedroom.

1. Should Amanda use a 6-inch ruler or a yardstick to measure the bookcase? Tell why you think so.
Check children's explanations.

page CC 70

Part B

The shelves in the bookcase are 16 inches high. Amanda wants to make sure her books will fit in the bookcase.

2. Find three different books in your classroom and measure their height.
Check children's measurements.
Book 1: _____ Book 2: _____ Book 3: _____

3. Which books that you measured will fit in Amanda's bookcase?
Check children's answers. Books should be less than 16 inches in height.

Explain how you know which books will fit.
Check children's explanations.

page CC 71

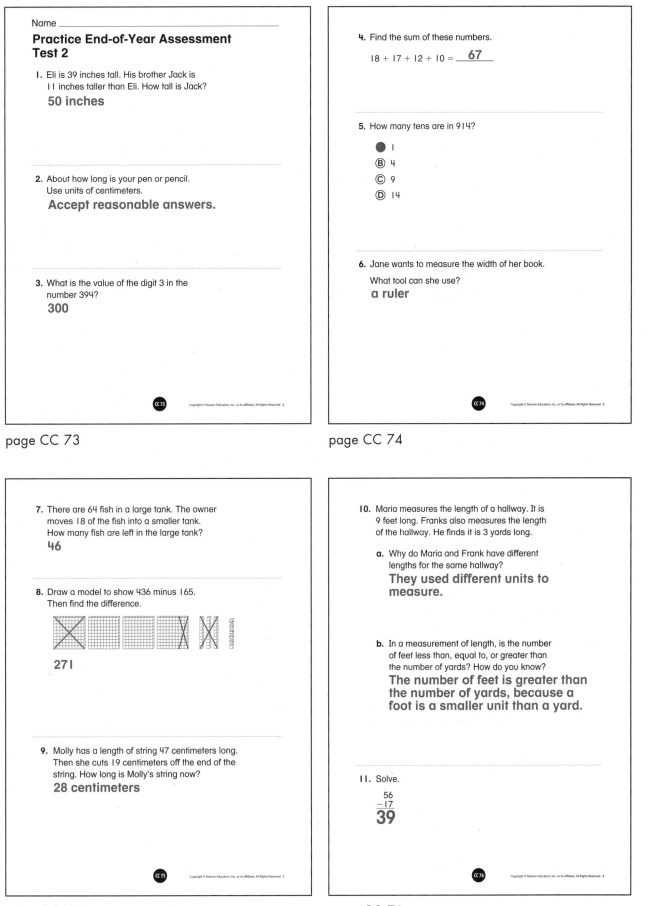

Name _____

Practice End-of-Year Assessment Test 2

1. Eli is 39 inches tall. His brother Jack is 11 inches taller than Eli. How tall is Jack?

50 inches

2. About how long is your pen or pencil. Use units of centimeters.

Accept reasonable answers.

3. What is the value of the digit 3 in the number 394?

300

page CC 73

---

4. Find the sum of these numbers.

18 + 17 + 12 + 10 = ___**67**___

5. How many tens are in 914?

● 1
Ⓑ 4
Ⓒ 9
Ⓓ 14

6. Jane wants to measure the width of her book. What tool can she use?

a ruler

page CC 74

---

7. There are 64 fish in a large tank. The owner moves 18 of the fish into a smaller tank. How many fish are left in the large tank?

46

8. Draw a model to show 436 minus 165. Then find the difference.

271

9. Molly has a length of string 47 centimeters long. Then she cuts 19 centimeters off the end of the string. How long is Molly's string now?

28 centimeters

page CC 75

---

10. Maria measures the length of a hallway. It is 9 feet long. Franks also measures the length of the hallway. He finds it is 3 yards long.

   a. Why do Maria and Frank have different lengths for the same hallway?
   They used different units to measure.

   b. In a measurement of length, is the number of feet less than, equal to, or greater than the number of yards? How do you know?
   The number of feet is greater than the number of yards, because a foot is a smaller unit than a yard.

11. Solve.

   56
   −17
   39

page CC 76

12. Stella has the coins shown below.

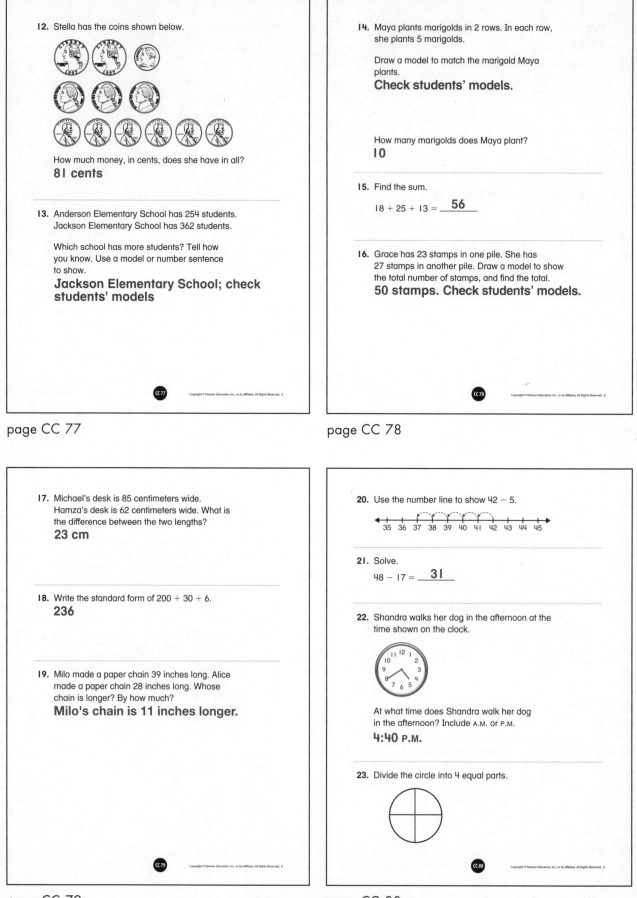

How much money, in cents, does she have in all?
81 cents

13. Anderson Elementary School has 254 students. Jackson Elementary School has 362 students.

Which school has more students? Tell how you know. Use a model or number sentence to show.
Jackson Elementary School; check students' models

page CC 77

14. Maya plants marigolds in 2 rows. In each row, she plants 5 marigolds.

Draw a model to match the marigold Maya plants.
Check students' models.

How many marigolds does Maya plant?
10

15. Find the sum.

$18 + 25 + 13 =$ ___**56**___

16. Grace has 23 stamps in one pile. She has 27 stamps in another pile. Draw a model to show the total number of stamps, and find the total.
50 stamps. Check students' models.

page CC 78

17. Michael's desk is 85 centimeters wide. Hamza's desk is 62 centimeters wide. What is the difference between the two lengths?
23 cm

18. Write the standard form of 200 + 30 + 6.
236

19. Milo made a paper chain 39 inches long. Alice made a paper chain 28 inches long. Whose chain is longer? By how much?
Milo's chain is 11 inches longer.

page CC 79

20. Use the number line to show 42 − 5.

35 36 37 38 39 40 41 42 43 44 45

21. Solve.

$48 - 17 =$ ___**31**___

22. Shandra walks her dog in the afternoon at the time shown on the clock.

At what time does Shandra walk her dog in the afternoon? Include A.M. or P.M.
4:40 P.M.

23. Divide the circle into 4 equal parts.

page CC 80

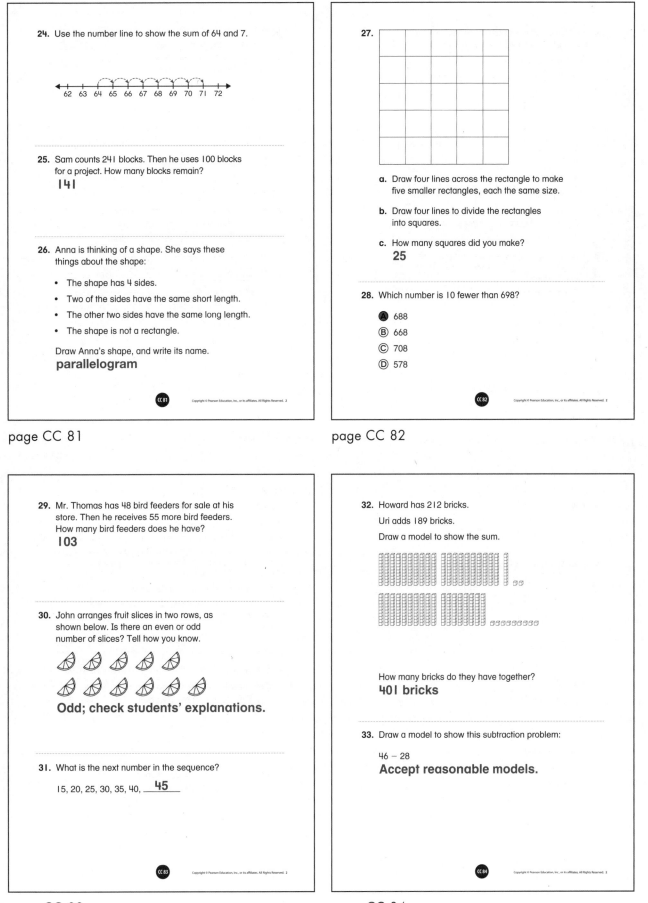

24. Use the number line to show the sum of 64 and 7.

62 63 64 65 66 67 68 69 70 71 72

25. Sam counts 241 blocks. Then he uses 100 blocks for a project. How many blocks remain?
141

26. Anna is thinking of a shape. She says these things about the shape:

- The shape has 4 sides.
- Two of the sides have the same short length.
- The other two sides have the same long length.
- The shape is not a rectangle.

Draw Anna's shape, and write its name.
parallelogram

page CC 81

27.

a. Draw four lines across the rectangle to make five smaller rectangles, each the same size.

b. Draw four lines to divide the rectangles into squares.

c. How many squares did you make?
25

28. Which number is 10 fewer than 698?

Ⓐ 688
Ⓑ 668
Ⓒ 708
Ⓓ 578

page CC 82

29. Mr. Thomas has 48 bird feeders for sale at his store. Then he receives 55 more bird feeders. How many bird feeders does he have?
103

30. John arranges fruit slices in two rows, as shown below. Is there an even or odd number of slices? Tell how you know.

Odd; check students' explanations.

31. What is the next number in the sequence?

15, 20, 25, 30, 35, 40, __**45**__

page CC 83

32. Howard has 212 bricks.

Uri adds 189 bricks.

Draw a model to show the sum.

How many bricks do they have together?
401 bricks

33. Draw a model to show this subtraction problem:

46 − 28
Accept reasonable models.

page CC 84

34. In which group does each figure belong? Write the letter of the figure in the correct box.

Sample:

No equal parts	2 equal parts	4 equal parts
A	D	B

Figure A   Figure B   Figure C   Figure D

35. Divide the rectangle below into 2 equal rows and 3 equal columns. How many squares are in the rectangle?

6 squares

page CC 85

36. The students in Ms. O'Neil's class run around the field. The tally chart shows how many times three students run around the field.

Stella	|||
Marge	|||||	
Jeff	|||||

Complete the picture graph to match the tally chart.

Laps Run

Stella ○ ○ ○
Marge ○ ○ ○ ○ ○
Jeff ○ ○ ○ ○ ○

0 1 2 3 4 5 6 7
○ = 1 Lap

37. Sara asks classmates how many pets they have. The data table shows the results.

Number of Pets	Number of Children
0	1
1	6
2	3
3	1
4	2

Draw Xs to show Sara's data on a line plot.

```
          ×
          ×
          ×
      ×   ×
      ×   ×       ×
  ×   ×   ×   ×   ×
——+———+———+———+———+———+———+——
  0   1   2   3   4   5   6
```

page CC 86

38. Find the sum.

$32 + 49 = \boxed{81}$

39. Complete each inequality. Tell with words or a model how you know which number is less.

487 _____ 478   709 _____ 712

40. Which of these is equal to 19? Circle Yes or No.

9 + 9	Yes	(No)
11 + 8	(Yes)	No
6 + 13	(Yes)	No
15 + 4	(Yes)	No

page CC 87

Name _____

Performance Task 3

Part A

Jimmy and his father love football. They always go to the high school football games. Their team is the Cougars. Jimmy wants to know how many people go to the Cougars' games.

At Game 1 of the Cougars' football season, there are between 500 and 600 people at the game.

1. Write a number that could be the number of people at Game 1.

There are _____ fans at Game 1.

Accept any number between 500 and 600.

2. Draw a model to show this number.
Check students' models.

3. Write the number in expanded form.
Check students' work.

page CC 88

Part B

Between 600 and 700 people come to the Cougars' Game 2.

4. Write a number that could be the number of people at Game 2.

There are _____ fans at Game 2.

Accept any number between 600 and 700.

5. Write a number sentence to compare the number of people at Game 1 with Game 2. Use your numbers.

Check students' inequality. They should have the number of people at Game 2 greater than the number of people at Game 1.

6. Are there more people at Game 2 than at Game 1? Explain how you know.

Yes, check students' explanations.

page CC 89

Performance Task 4
Part A

The students in Ms. Jones' second grade class set up a bird feeder outside their classroom. Every morning they count the number of birds at the bird feeder. The table shows the number of birds that the students counted in four days.

Day	Monday	Tuesday	Wednesday	Thursday
Number of Birds	11	7	10	9

1. Angie and Willa want to display the data they collect. Angie wants to make a bar graph. Willa wants to make a pictograph. Which type of graph should they make? Tell why you think so.

Check students' answers.

2. Draw a graph, either a bar graph or a pictograph, to show the data.

Check students' graphs.

Monday Tuesday Wednesday Thursday

page CC 90

Part B

Aldo and Emma compare the number of birds they counted.

Aldo says that they counted more birds on Monday and Tuesday combined than on Wednesday and Thursday combined.

Emma says they counted fewer birds on Monday and Tuesday combined than on Wednesday and Thursday combined.

3. Who do you agree with? Tell why. Use models or equations in your answer.

Check students' answers and models.

page CC 91

Practice End-of-Year Assessments Correlation Chart

Test 1 and Test 2

The chart below provides information about the two Practice End-of-Year Assessments, Test 1, found in the students' workbook and Test 2, a secure version, found in this Teacher's Guide, starting on page CC 73. The chart lists the Standard for Mathematical Content that is the primary assessment focus of each item. It also indicates whether the standard assessed is a major, supporting or additional content emphasis (as determined by both PARCC and SBAC). Finally, the last column points to the lesson(s) in enVisionMATH Common Core where students can be directed if they need additional practice or review of concepts.

Item Test 1 and Test 2	CCSS	Content Emphasis	enVisionMATH Common Core Lessons	Investigations Units.
1	2.MD.5	Major	15-7	U9 Inv. 1; U9 Inv. 2
2	2.MD.3	Supporting	15-2, 15-3, 15-4, 15-5	U9 Inv. 3
3	2.NBT.1	Major	10-2	U6 Inv. 5A
4	2.NBT.6	Major	8-7	U6 Inv. 3; U8 Inv. 4
5	2.NBT.1	Major	10-2	U6 Inv. 5A
6	2.MD.1	Supporting	15-1, 15-2, 15-3, 15-4, 15-5	U9 Inv. 2
7	2.OA.1	Major	8-9	U1 Inv. 4; U3 Inv. 2; U8 Inv. 3
8	2.NBT.7	Major	11-8	U8 Inv. 5A
9	2.OA.1	Major	8-9	U1 Inv. 4; U3 Inv. 2; U8 Inv. 3
10	2.MD.2	Supporting	15-6	U9 Inv. 1
11	2.NBT.5	Major	9-5	U3 Inv. 2; U6 Inv. 2; U8 Inv. 3
12	2.MD.8	Additional	13-1, 13-2	U6 Inv. 3; U6 Inv. 4
13	2.NBT.4	Major	10-1, 10-7	U6 Inv. 5A
14	2.OA.4	Supporting	4-1, 4-2, 4-4	U5 Inv. 1
15	2.NBT.6	Major	8-7	U6 Inv. 3; U8 Inv. 4
16	2.OA.1	Major	9-4, 9-5	U1 Inv. 4; U3 Inv. 2; U8 Inv. 4
17	2.MD.5	Major	15-7, 15-8, 15-9	U9 Inv. 1; U9 Inv. 2
18	2.NBT.3	Supporting	10-3	U1 Inv. 2; U6 Inv. 5A
19	2.MD.5	Major	15-7, 15-8, 15-9	U9 Inv. 1; U9 Inv. 2
20	2.NBT.9	Major	9-6	U6 Inv. 1; U8 Inv. 3

Item Test 1 and Test 2	CCSS	Content Emphasis	enVisionMATH Common Core Lessons	Investigations Units.
21	2.NBT.5	Major	9-5	U3 Inv. 2; U6 Inv. 2; U8 Inv. 3
22	2.MD.7	Additional	16-1	U2 Inv. 2
23	2.G.3	Major	12-7	U7 Inv. 2
24	2.NBT.9	Major	8-6	U6 Inv. 1; U6 Inv. 2; U8 Inv. 4
25	2.NBT.8	Major	11-2	U6 Inv. 5A
26	2.G.1	Supporting	12-3	U2 Inv. 1
27	2.G.2	Major	12-6	U2 Inv. 2
28	2.NBT.8	Major	11-2	U6 Inv. 5A
29	2.MD.8	Major	14-2	U6 Inv. 3
30	2.OA.3	Additional	5-6	U8 Inv. 1
31	2.NBT.2	Supporting	10-6	U3 Inv. 3; U5 Inv. 1; U5 Inv. 2
32	2.NBT.7	Major	11-3	U8 Inv. 5A
33	2.OA.1	Major	9-4	U1 Inv. 4; U3 Inv. 2; U8 Inv. 3
34	2.G.3	Major	12-7	U7 Inv. 1; U7 Inv. 2
35	2.G.2	Major	12-6	U2 Inv. 2
36	2.MD.10	Supporting	16-5	U4 Inv. 1; U4 Inv. 2
37	2.MD.9	Supporting	16-4	U9 Inv. 1
38	2.NBT.5	Major	8-5	U3 Inv. 2; U8 Inv. 4
39	2.NBT.4	Major	10-1, 10-7	U6 Inv. 5A
40	2.OA.2	Major	2-2, 2-3, 2-6	U1 Inv. 3; U1 Inv. 4

Performance Tasks Scoring Rubrics

Performance Task 1

Primary Content Domains and Clusters

Operations and Algebraic Thinking: Represent and solve problems involving addition and subtraction. (2.OA.1); Work with equal groups of objects to gain foundation for multiplication. (2.OA.3, 2.OA.4)

Secondary Content Domains and Clusters

Number and Operations in Base Ten: Use place value understanding and properties of operations to add and subtract. (2.NBT.5)

Math Practices Focus

MP 1, 2, 4, 7

Scoring Rubric

1	Determines the number of boxes of oranges sold in all.	6
	Adds the amount sold in the two weeks.	
	Explains how to add the two numbers.	
2	Explains how to find the number of oranges.	5
	Describes a counting, or addition process.	
3	Finds the number of oranges in a box.	3
	Multiplies, adds, or counts correctly.	
4	Shows understanding of even and odd numbers.	6
	Notes that the number is even.	
	Explains why the number is even.	
TOTAL		20

Performance Task 2

Primary Content Domains and Clusters

Measurement and Data: Measure and estimate length in standard units. (2.MD.1, 2.MD.3, 2.MD.4)

Secondary Content Domains and Clusters

Number and Operations in Base Ten: Understand place value. (2.NBT.4)

Math Practices Focus

MP 1, 2, 5, 6

Scoring Rubric

1	Chooses appropriate tool to measure.	6
	Justifies the choice of measurement tool.	
2	Measure height of three different books	6
	Accurately measures height of book 1.	
	Accurately measures height of book 2.	
	Accurately measures height of book 3.	
3	Finds and explains which books will fit.	8
	Chooses only the books that are less than 16 inches.	
	Explains which books fit in the bookcase.	
TOTAL		20

Performance Task 3

Primary Content Domains and Clusters

Operations and Algebraic Thinking: Understand place value. (2.NBT.3, 2.NBT.4)

Math Practices Focus

MP 1, 2, 4, 7, 8

Scoring Rubric

1	**Chooses an appropriate number.**	2
	Writes a number between 500 and 600.	
2	**Draws accurate model of number.**	4
	Shows a model that clearly represents the answer in part 1.	
3	**Writes number in expanded form.**	4
	Writes number from part 1 as correct sum in expanded form.	
4	**Chooses an appropriate number.**	2
	Writes a number between 600 and 700.	
5	**Writes a correct inequality.**	4
	Writes an inequality using numbers from parts 1 and 4.	
6	**Writes an explanation.**	4
	Shows why more people are at Game 2.	
TOTAL		**20**

Performance Task 4

Primary Content Domains and Clusters

Measurement and Data: Represent and interpret data. (2.MD.10)

Secondary Content Domains and Clusters

Operations and Algebraic Thinking: Represent and solve problems involving addition and subtraction. (2.OA.1); Add and subtract within 20. (2.OA.2)

Math Practices Focus

MP 1, 2, 3, 8

Scoring Rubric

1	**Chooses an appropriate graph.**	4
	Justifies the choice of graph.	
2	**Draws an accurate graph.**	8
	Accurately shows the amount for each column of the graph.	
3	**Justifies correct answer using models or equations.**	8
	Agrees with Emma.	
	Justifies answer using models or equations.	
TOTAL		20